Reader V

"I could r
of the essc
insights each time. ... A great book to review,
more than once!" – Susan Violante, *Reader*
Views

National Indie Excellence Awards
Mind Body Spirit Finalist

"I love this little book! ... Carry this book
with you, read and reread the essays, and
connect with joy. " – Kathryn Lanier,
InnerChange magazine

Sacramento Publisher's Assn. Awards
Best Nonfiction & Best Spiritual book

"He writes beautifully, clearly, elegantly
... he is incapable of an unoriginal
thought." – Joseph Polansky, *Diamond*
Fire magazine

USA Book News Best Books Awards
Mind Body Spirit Finalist

"It's a beautiful little book to carry around
for when you just want something to read at
odd moments, but I suspect that, for some, it
will be a book that's picked up over and over
again. ... I highly recommend this book to anyone with an
open mind and a real willingness to look at themselves and
their surroundings." – J Byrne, *Psychic-Magic* magazine

Bob Makransky's **Introduction to Magic** Series:

"In this series, not only do we get an author who knows his subject inside out, but also a directness of approach not often seen in works of this kind. Not for Makransky the wishy-washy approach that attempts to soothe and reassure the reader with false promises of magical success - something about which many customer complaints arise on the Amazon website - but, rather, an honest and uncompromising study of what Magic really entails. – James Lynn Page (author of *Celtic Magic, Everyday Tarot* and *The Christ Enigma*)

What is Magic?, the introductory book on witchcraft, Paperback $17.95: **www.createspace.com/4780367**

Magical Living, about paganism, Paperback $14.95: **www.createspace.com/4780358**

Thought Forms, about cognitive psychology and the Mercury cycle, Paperback $19.95: **www.createspace.com/4770114**

The Great Wheel, about reincarnation and the lunar cycle, ebook $9.95: **www.smashwords.com/books/view/306020**
Kindle edition: **www.amzn.com/B00CD958PS**

* * * * *

Topics in Astrology Paperback $19.95
www.createspace.com/5712718

Planetary Strength Paperback £11.99
www.amzn.com/1902405501

Planetary Combination Paperback £17.50
www.amzn.com/1910531103

Planetary Hours Paperback £11.00
www.amzn.com/1910531057

Magical Living

Essays for the New Age

Volume II of the *Introduction to Magic* series

by Bob Makransky

ISBN-13: 978-1499279337 ISBN-10: 1499279337

Makransky, Bob
  Magical Living --: essays for the New Age / by
  Bob Makransky. – 2nd ed.
      p. cm
      LCCN: 00-130616
  1. New Age Movement. 2. Magic. 3. Occultism.
  I. Title.

      BP605.N48M35 2001
      QBI00-380

      Published by Dear Brutus Press
      https://www.createspace.com/4780358

Contents

Acknowledgments

Quotations from *Man's Search for Meaning* by Viktor E. Frankl copyright 1959, 1962, 1984, 1992 by Viktor E. Frankl are reprinted by permission of Beacon Press, Boston.

Quotation from *Agriculture – a Course of Eight Lectures* by Rudolf Steiner copyright 1974 by the Bio-Dynamic Agricultural Association is reprinted by permission of the Bio-Dynamic Farming and Gardening Association, San Francisco.

Photographs from the Carl Van Vechten Collection of the Library of Congress, Prints & Photographs Division.

Most of these essays originally appeared in *Diamond Fire* magazine, and thanks are due to Joseph Polansky for permission to publish them here. I would also like to thank Dany Bouchard, Darron and Karen Collins, Milly Hernandez, Janeen Simon, and Bob Wachtel for their perceptive critique and suggestions.

Preface

There are three paths to the Spirit: control over the body (e.g., hatha yoga); control over the mind (e.g., insight meditation); and control over the emotions. The practice of magic aims at control of the emotions; its goal is to arrive at a place where one is perfectly content and at ease in the now moment – neither angry about the past nor fearful of the future. When the emotions have calmed down, the body and mind naturally relax as well.

My approach to the subject of magic in these essays is necessarily based upon my own personal experience, which may not be the same as yours or someone else's. For example, what I say about evil spirits is congruent with my own personal experiences with them: what I say about them is factually correct, but is based upon my own facts. Another person with a different set of experiences and expectations will probably come to somewhat different conclusions. In other words, when we leave the world of ordinary society and strike out on our own to become magicians, we also leave behind a body of common experience and consensual validation which average people rely upon to orient themselves. To become a magician is to deliberately seek disorienting stimuli. There are no real guidelines or guiderails or anything solid to hang onto beyond one's own will, determination, and the wisdom born of experience. Therefore, the information given in these essays should not be taken as gospel or chiseled into stone. It was channeled to me for my own guidance, and it is based loosely on Carlos Castaneda's worldview, since that is the model my spirit guides used in explaining things to me. There are other praxes (such as Franz Bardon's) which are based upon different worldviews and which are equally valid. The reader who desires a more complete theoretical exposition of what magic is and how it works, and a more formal course of magical training and practice, is referred to my book *Thought Forms*, also available from Dear Brutus Press.

This second (2014) Edition omits the Tables of Planetary Hours included in the first edition, since the existence of the free downloadable Planetary Hours Calculator (an Excel worksheet) posted at: http://www.dearbrutus.com/body_ planetaryhours.html has superseded printed tables; although printed tables for all latitudes from 58° North latitude to 58° South latitude are available in my book *Planetary Hours*. To compensate, this second edition of *Magical Living* includes some extra sections not found in the first edition: a few extra chapters, and the Appendix with some selections and explanations from *Thought Forms*.

B. M.

Channeling Spirit Guides

Glendower: *"I can call spirits from the vasty deep."*
Hotspur: *"Why, so can I, or so can any man;*
               But will they come when you do call for them?"
                            Henry IV, Part I

    Like that character from Moliere who was delighted to learn that he'd been speaking prose all along and never knew it, each and every one of us is channeling all the time; and the only difference between "professional" psychics and mediums and the rest of us is that the psychics are aware of what they're doing – they make a special point of (call special attention to) a completely natural process that everybody already knows how to do. Everyone has spirit guides who talk to them constantly; however, most people don't listen to these messages, any more than they listen to what other people – such as their parents, spouse, or children – are trying to tell them. When a thought or feeling prompted by a spirit guide pops up in their consciousness, they just pass over it or reject it. In this essay we will discuss thought forms, spirit guides, and other beings which can be channeled, together with a simple technique for consciously channeling them.

    In order to get an idea of what spirits are, it is first necessary to get a handle on what *we* are. Contrary to popular opinion, we are not solid, abiding objects that have individual self-existence. Although it certainly appears that the world is "real" and consists of solid, discrete objects, in fact our world is more like a movie screen, hooked up to other people's movie screens, on which we're all projecting what we're feeling inside outwards as symbols – solid objects in a physical world.

    To ask Heidegger's question, "Why are there things rather than nothing?" is like asking, "Why can't soccer players use their hands? Why did God so construct the universe that soccer players can't use their hands?" In the same way, our perception of the universe as a world of solid, discrete objects is a wholly man-made restriction on our senses. Plants and animals don't perceive the world in this fashion, and neither, for that matter, do infants and lunatics. They still use their "hands" (their feelings rather than their minds) to play the game of perception. As a result, they don't "play soccer" very well, but they still have the free use of their hands – their intuition – which most people have learned to repress. The belief that we are discrete entities in a world of solid objects is just that – a belief – that makes the world of concepts, of thinking, possible.

Admittedly, the belief that we are discrete, abiding entities in a world of solid objects certainly seems to be true most of the time we are awake – it's a pretty convincing belief. But that's only because we have the door tightly shut on any evidence that contradicts this belief. That door is called "fear of going crazy or of being thought crazy." Keeping our sanity is equivalent to screening out lots of information about ourselves and the world around us which would be available if we could just loosen up a bit and drop the pretense that we exist as solid objects.

In fact, our existence is multidimensional. We not only exist in an infinite number of past and future lives, but we are also infinitely ramified in all the probable realities which branch off from this present lifetime. Every time we make a decision – big or little – we create a probable reality in which that decision was made, and another or other probable realities in which that decision wasn't made. For example, that person whom you wistfully smiled at from afar once but never spoke to nor saw again, is your spouse in another probable reality in which you *did* go over and strike up a conversation.

Thus, not only does the totality of who "we" are encompass infinite lifetimes in other worlds and realities, it also encompasses infinite probable realities within this present lifetime as well as all those others. Not only that, but within the confines of a single probable reality of a single lifetime, which is all we normally pay attention to or consider to be "ourselves", we are still multiple personalities. That is to say, we are not the same person from moment to moment, but in fact shift from one to another subpersonalities or thought forms in response to this or that changing stimulus. The only difference between an Eve, Sybil, or Truddi and the rest of us is that their slips are showing: they're acting out the multiple personality role openly, whereas the rest of us are marching around with our dress uniforms – our fear of going crazy – buttoned down tight.

Most of what we consider to be "ourselves" – that is, the thoughts, feelings and perceptions which occupy our conscious minds most of the time we are awake; our sense that there is a continuing "us" there – is just a collection of habits and predilections learned from our parents and society. Each of our habitual thoughts, moods, beliefs, etc. is a thought form – a learned behavior which is a being in its own right (some authors, such as Richard Dawkins and Daniel Dennett, have used the term *memes* instead of *thought forms*). Most of what we think *we* think, believe, or perceive is actually just what our parents and society think, believe, or perceive; and these thoughts, beliefs, and perceptions have an awareness, a sense of selfhood, and a will to live all their own. We create them with our decisions and we breathe the breath of life into them with our attention.

Basically, every time we think a thought we are channeling a thought form. However, this is an unskillful way of channeling because it's mindless. Thought forms grab our attention and say, "Think this! Think that! Think the other! In response to this, do that! Remember this! Desire that! Blah blah blah!" all day long every day. Thought forms are our automatic pilot – although we ourselves create them, we are subject to their control thereafter. We go along and just think whatever our thought forms want us to think. It rarely occurs to us to stop and ask, "Why? Why am I thinking this thought? Is entertaining this thought going to benefit me? From whence does this thought arise? At what point in my life did I first begin entertaining this thought? When did I make it a part of my inventory of habitual thoughts? Etc."

To ask these sorts of questions (and pay attention to the answers) is called active imagination, and it is a more functional form of channeling thought forms than is normal thinking. Active imagination is a technique invented by Carl Jung, and it is described at great length in my book *Thought Forms*. In active imagination we interact with our thought forms, whereas in normal thinking we just snap to and salute whenever a thought form barks a command at us. Active imagination is facilitated by automatic writing (which we shall learn how to do presently); i.e. automatic writing is a refinement of the technique of active imagination, but it's by no means the only way to do it. Thoughtful, introspective people are doing active imagination all the time without calling it that or giving any special attention to it; but, in fact, active imagination is a wholly different form of channeling thought forms than is normal thinking.

So thought forms – habitual patterns of thought picked up from our parents and society – account for most of what we consider "our" thoughts and feelings; and spirits – both good and evil – account for most of what's left. The chief difference between thought forms and spirits is that thought forms are within us, created by us, a part of us; whereas spirits are outside of us. When we channel (e.g. by automatic writing) we run across a whole menagerie of entities – both thought forms and different kinds of spirits – so it's helpful to know the differences between these various kinds of beings.

There are lots of different kinds of spirits in the world. We are spirits, for that matter. Some spirits are entirely useless to humans – we cannot even communicate with such entities. Others are nasty little things which are best avoided altogether. And still others can be quite helpful to humans, for a multitude of purposes.

The use of nature spirits, such as water spirits, to wash away our self-importance and help us tune in to our true feelings of joy and peace with the world, will be described in a later essay. The use of tree spirits is described at length in my book *Thought Forms*.

There are also spirits which oversee particular human activities such as agriculture, art, construction, cooking, healing, mathematics, mining, etc. etc. Every human endeavor has a cadre of spirits proper to it, which guides individual practitioners and also helps humanity as a whole expand its knowledge of the various arts, crafts, and sciences. A competent, inspired professional in any field is constantly receiving inspiration and new ideas from the spirits who oversee his or her field. However, as is the case also with thought forms, most people believe that any inspiration they receive in this fashion is "their" idea, when in fact it's being passed to them by spirits. To be a competent professional in any field is to be a clear channel for the spirits who oversee that field.

Finally, we come to personal spirit guides – what some people call angels. These are spirits who are assigned to individual human beings, who tend them as wards. Everybody has at least one personal spirit guide at any one time, but most people have several or lots of them, which may come and go in the course of a lifetime.

Although both thought forms and spirit guides can be channeled in the same ways (as can other spirits: Jesus and Mary, Krishna, nature spirits, demons, recently deceased people, etc.), thought forms and spirit guides are completely different kinds of entities. Thought forms are created by us: they stand in the same relation to us that we stand to God. Guides, on the other hand, are a bit above us in the sense of being wiser, possessing broader viewpoints and more loving hearts, but they aren't that far above us.

Many spirit guides have had human incarnations. Sometimes deceased friends, relatives, ancestors, or even aborted fetuses become one's spirit guides; and one of my own guides has told me that there are lives / realities in which I am *her* spirit guide. I presume that similar relationships between people and their guides obtain for everyone.

Up until recently in human history (last few thousand years) magical knowledge – the practical application of intuition – was handed down from generation to generation, as agricultural or mathematical knowledge is. However, because of the nature of the times, most of that knowledge was lost as skilled practitioners died off without leaving heirs. In the interim, the White Brotherhood, the "guild" of spirit guides, came in to fill the gap – to steer humanity in more or less the right direction during its sleep-walking (materialistic) phase.

There's a great network spread out across the world now, a linking up of groups of spirits and human channels, sending out filaments of light around the earth to love it and heal it. To learn to consciously channel your spirit guides is to join this fraternity of light. As long as there is light, no evil can overcome the earth.

Now we will describe how to channel spirit guides by automatic writing. But it must be pointed out that automatic writing is just a way of making channeling deliberate or special, of endowing it with an aura of mystery. By distinguishing the process of channeling in this way it is easier to understand and learn – to learn in the sense of separating it out of normal thinking and feeling, and to understand when "our" thoughts and feelings indeed arise within ourselves, and when they are being passed to us by a spirit. Channeling can be done via normal thinking and feeling; in trance; in dreams; and by automatic writing. Automatic writing, albeit not as clear as trance channeling (more admixture of the person channeling in the final product), has the advantage of providing a written record of a spirit's messages – something which is often useful for future reference. A lot of things spirits say to us make more sense in retrospect.

I've personally taught some hundred people to channel their spirit guides, and of that number only half a dozen or so have blocked so badly that they couldn't do it. But nobody needs a teacher to learn something as easy and basic as channeling. The only function my presence as a teacher serves is to prop up my students' faith, to put their noses down to it: I have a rather overbearing personality that expects and assumes that people will channel successfully – which doesn't offer my students much margin for doubt or failure. But this is just a didactic device – I'm convinced that anyone who wants to channel can channel, with no need for a teacher.

It's best to tackle automatic writing when you have some pressing personal question to ask, or when you are moved by a burning curiosity to communicate with your spirit guides. Idle curiosity may not have enough oomph behind it to forge a clear communications link. The reason some people block conscious channeling (or reject the idea altogether) is that they don't want to face up to the fact that they are not solid, continuing, individual beings, but rather are a flux of thought forms (images, opinions, beliefs, and expectations learned from parents and society) being urged this way and that by spirit forces.

In other words, to open to channel means to lay aside a lot of common assumptions about the nature of personal existence; and some people find this frightening. If you find yourself blocking, just set the project aside until you have a dire need to question your guides – that need will be sufficient motivation to break the block. Like everything else in life, channeling comes more easily to some people than to others (e.g. to people with good Neptune aspects to their sun or moon); but anyone can channel if they just keep plugging away at it.

Choose a time when you are relaxed, alert, calm, and will not be interrupted. Being at a power tree or power spot is a *big* help. If you are into astrology, you can use a lunar planetary hour; however this is merely a help, not a necessity. Lie down or sit, as you prefer, with a pen and notebook in hand (although channeling can also be done on a typewriter or word processor). Writing down both your questions and the replies as they come in the form of a dialogue, ask your guides to please talk to you. For example, you might start this way:

Me: "My spirit guides, could you please come and talk to me? I am really trying to be open right now, and I want to hear what you have to say to me. I have this problem that I need an answer to; won't you please come and talk to me about it. Etc. etc."

This is just an example – you should ask your guides to talk to you using your own words and sentiments. Keep writing, keep on coaxing them, until you begin to feel an answer forming in your mind, and then write it down. The trick to making this work is to not stop writing. That's the purpose of the writing – to focus your attention on the act of writing, like when you're taking notes in a classroom, so that there's less room for doubt, hesitation, fear, etc. Keep on writing, even if you're just writing the same plea over and over again. Do make it heartfelt – not just done mechanically – and eventually you'll start getting an answer. It really is so simple and straightforward you won't believe it – "Look, ma, I'm channeling!"

Note that when a person channels for the first time, the answers tend to come out sort of inchoate and constipated. Don't worry – just push it right on out and don't worry about whether it makes sense or not. Usually in automatic writing a few words or phrases spring into your mind at a time, a little faster than you can write them down, though sometimes you might get whole blocks or paragraphs at once. You might also see memory pictures pop up before your mind's eye, or get flashes of dream-like scenes as you write. Record all of this because it's all relevant. Something might not make sense at the moment, but it will eventually if you keep a written record of it.

If nothing comes to mind in response to your entreaties; or if all that comes to mind is gibberish; then you are blocking. Your conscious mind might say, "This isn't working. I'm not doing it right." or "There must be some trick to this!" in its effort to subvert the process. Don't fall for that ploy! Keep trying, keep on writing, even if all you get is gibberish. Only trust can open you enough to write automatically; otherwise you tangle yourself with doubt. Doubt is the enemy of all magic, and it can completely tear down automatic writing at the outset. Faith is the key to success here, as elsewhere, and a strong curiosity is a valuable asset as well. Bear in mind that your spirit guides will be thrilled to open this channel of communication with you, and they will do everything they can, from their side, to assist you. If you find yourself blocking, try switching to your non-dominant hand; or do it standing on your head (leaning against a wall). Keep on writing, and at some moment your conscious mind will relax its grip and you'll start writing automatically. Then, simply write down what your spirit guides tell you, asking any questions you like along the way.

Ask your guides what their names are, and if they have specific messages for you. Some people "see" their spirit guides in their mind's eye; though I've never seen my guides in this manner, I have met them in dreams. In automatic writing (as opposed to trance channeling) there is a lot of medium thrown in with the message. One of my spirit guides is also channeled by several other people, and while you can tell that it's the same entity coming through, she sounds different through each of us. For one thing, she speaks in English to those whose native language is English, and in Spanish to those of Spanish tongue. Beyond that, her diction, outlook, interests, etc. mirror those of the person channeling her. What is invariant from channel to channel is her feeling – the sense of her presence – and the tenor and direction of her thinking. But her relationships with her various channels are as diverse as the channels are.

It's difficult to generalize about spirit guides – each is different, as people are different. They will speak to us in a manner we are capable of understanding: they address us according to where we are coming from, in terms we are capable of receiving. If there's something we just don't want to hear, it's easy enough to block it, just as we tend to block out what we don't want to hear from other people. Sometimes my own guides have had to wait until I was in a particularly relaxed or unguarded frame of mind to sock something to me that I didn't want to hear. And at times I've remonstrated, "Why didn't you tell me this before?"; to which their usual rejoinder is, "We were telling you all along, but you refused to listen!"

Once you've got the technique of automatic writing down pat, you can use it to channel any spirits, not just your personal guides. This means nature spirits, recently deceased people, even Jesus, Mary, Krishna, Buddha, saints, etc. God can't be channeled this way, however, because God doesn't "talk". If you get a message purporting to come from God, it's some wise-guy spirit putting you on. Automatic writing can also be used as part of active imagination (Carl Jung's technique for doing inner work – self-analysis for self-transformation. See my book *Thought Forms* for details). You may wonder how you can tell if you're channeling evil spirits. All I can say is that all of the evil spirits which I've run across in my channeling made no bones about who they were or what they were up to. Evil spirits seek willing accomplices – they need a decision on your part to commit evil, they can't trick you against your will. However, they can come up with some pretty tempting offers sometimes. I would say, though, that if the messages you are channeling are full of fulsome praise at how marvelous you are, and pity at how misunderstood you are, and how much you have to suffer, then probably you're channeling demons. Real spirit guides will buck you up when you are feeling low; but they'll also kick you in the butt if you indulge in self-pity. Their actual goal is to get you to a place where you have your own true feelings working, so that you don't need them anymore.

Okay, now you're a professional, dyed-in-the-wool spirit channel, ready to hang out your shingle and charge for readings. Now what?

Generally speaking, spirit guides are useless for calling horse races, lottery numbers, or even for predicting the outcome of specific events. If prediction is what you want, it's better to use horary astrology, tarot, etc. than to ask of your guides. My experience is that spirit guides can predict the outcome of certain events when they volunteer the information; but they can't or won't predict outcomes merely at our behest. This is because spirit guides look at things very differently from us; they're on another wavelength, and the things which are of crucial importance to us are not of consequence to them. Spirits don't give a hang about what we call the "future", and they regard our obsession with it as an odd peculiarity of our species, scarcely worthy of serious notice. On the other hand, things that spirits believe should be simple for us (such as dropping lifelong habits, addictions, fears, etc. as a simple act of will) in fact present insuperable difficulties which spirits can't really appreciate. Even spirits who have had human incarnations tend to forget what it's like down here. Things just aren't as simple as they try to make them seem, because they don't have to deal with doubt, fear, inertia, temptation, taxes, etc.

Nor are spirit guides capable of pulling our chestnuts out of the fire for us, saving our skins, or changing the outward circumstances of our lives. There are spirits which can assist us with the concrete problems of our lives to some extent, but spirit guides are basically advisors, not employees.

Spirit guides can't live our lives for us; they can't feel our feelings for us, can't absorb or deflect our pain for us, can't resolve our problems for us, and can't find our happiness for us. All they can do is show us how to take responsibility for doing these things ourselves.

What We Can Learn From Plants

This young woman knew that she would die in the next few days.   But when I talked to her she was cheerful in spite of this knowledge.   "I am grateful that fate has hit me so hard," she told me.   "In my former life I was spoiled and did not take spiritual accomplishments seriously."   Pointing through the window of the hut, she said, "This tree here is the only friend I have in my loneliness."   Through that window she could see just one branch of a chestnut tree, and on the branch were two blossoms.   "I often talk to this tree," she said to me.   I was startled and didn't quite know how to take her words.   Was she delirious?   Did she have occasional hallucinations?   Anxiously I asked her if the tree replied.   "Yes."   What did it say to her?   She answered, "It said to me, 'I am here – I am here – I am life, eternal life.'"

    – Viktor Frankl, *Man's Search for Meaning*

What we can learn from plants is how to be joyous. We can't learn that from other people, usually, because the setup with other people isn't to be joyous; on the contrary, it is to be fearful, close-hearted, and uptight. Therefore, to learn to be joyous, we have to go to the plants. If we can first learn to be joyous from the plants – who aren't out to cause us grief – we can then learn to be joyous with our fellow humans.

Of course, the joy we receive from plants doesn't have all the ego zing of a sexy partner, or a mother's approval, or the boss's congratulations; but it's always there. That's the nice thing. No matter how horribly our lives are going, or how much rejection other people heap upon us, the plants are always there being happy.

At a nearby airport there is a hedge in front of the entrance for departing passengers, and when the wind blows across the hedge the shrubs wave "Bye-bye! Bon Voyage! Feliz Viaje!" to all the passengers. Nobody pays any attention to them, but the plants don't care. They don't need people's acknowledgment and validation to be happy. They're just there, pouring love out into the world. That's their job, and the people passing by receive that love whether they're consciously aware of it or not. The plants are what keep this from being a hell world. There are no plants in a hell world. The plants in this world are not just the bottom of the food chain; they're anchoring all of us uptight animals to the earth's love. They aren't just the source of all our oxygen; they're the source of all our joy. They just sit there casting joy out all over the place.

What we can learn from plants is that there is love surrounding us all the time, every minute, had we but the wit to see it, feel it. We are being offered love all the time, but we reject it because we don't understand that's what love is. We think love should be zappier, instead of quiet and peaceful and waving in the wind.

The love which plants offer us – the sound of leaves rustling, the smell of pine needles – is all there is. This is not a poetic metaphor: it's a cold, hard fact of life. If we want / need / desire something to make us happy beyond what the plants offer us, then we're just out of luck, because that's all there is. If we can't find happiness in what's going on outside our windows right this minute, then we're just out of luck.

To tune into plants is quite simple. First of all, you must have the conviction that there is indeed something you can learn from plants. You can't go in there with the attitude that you're better, smarter, or superior to a plant. We're all taught that we're superior to plants, just as we're taught that we're superior to other people. And just as we don't pay much attention to the people we think we're superior to, we can't tune into the feelings of plants if we think we're superior to them. It isn't hard to overcome this prejudice if we just bear in mind that in the only thing that really matters in life – being joyous unto one's self – plants have it all over us humans.

Go to the plants every single day, for at least fifteen minutes or half an hour. Go sit out under a tree – perhaps during lunch break. It's better to make such a space for yourself during the day, as a break from the buzz-buzz, but do it at night if you can't find time during the day. But go every day, preferably alone, without fail. Make it the most important item on your agenda – that this brief time you take for yourself with the plants is inviolable. If you make such a firm decision – that being joyous is an unalterable priority in your life – then the joy itself will follow naturally.

No specific instructions are needed on where you should go or what you should do there. If there's some specific tree or woods or meadow that calls your attention, then go there. If not, just go where you feel like going, or where you conveniently can go. Get away from people, if possible, and do what you feel like doing. There is no particular procedure, and you should have no particular expectations. Maybe the plants will start talking to you; if you ask them to nicely, they will. If not, you may never feel anything out of the ordinary except for a subtle feeling of relaxation, a general lightening up of your entire life, as time goes on.

What the plants are offering us is true love, if we take the trouble to avail ourselves of it. They will give it to us whether we feel what they are doing to us or not, whether we are consciously aware of it or not. So don't worry if you can't seem to feel with the plants in the beginning. All you have to do is to make a firm commitment to put yourself under their tutelage, and they will find a way to do the rest.

Be assured that the plants are actually acting on you. It takes a while to pick up the thread of what they're doing to you, but after a while you find they can calm you down and soothe you, no matter what kind of frenzy is going on in your world of people.

In other words, the interactions we have with plants are of a different order than the interactions we have going on with people. We interact with plants on an intuitive level, a feeling level; whereas we interact with other people on a thought form level (of images, expectations, defenses, competition, etc.). Most of us have forgotten how to relate on a feeling level, but the plants themselves will teach us how to do this if we make a serious effort to learn, in a day-by-day fashion.

You can't expect immediate results, but surely after six or eight months of going to the plants every day you should at least be beginning to understand what the plants are doing to you. When you get to the place where your hiatus with the plants is the high point of your daily routine – the part of your day which you most eagerly anticipate – then you can be said to have arrived: to understand what we can learn from plants.

Communicating With Plants

Plants' experience of being in the world is very different from the experience of us animals. Because plants cannot move about, they exist in a state of profound acceptance and peace within themselves. Emotions such as fear, hate, jealousy, possessiveness, etc. are wholly unknown to plants and would serve no useful purpose. On the other hand, plants are capable of experiencing a wide range of higher emotions the like of which we animals could scarcely conceive.

At the same time, there are feelings which plants share with us animals, such as love, pain, joy, thirst, etc. It is the feelings we share with plants which provide the basis of our ability to communicate with them.

Feeling with plants is not so different from feeling with people. For example, when we are about to have sex with someone who really turns us on, we feel a palpable surge of sexual energy connecting us to that person. Similarly, when we walk into a room to face someone who is madder than hell at us, we feel connected to that person by a palpable wave of anger and fear. When a baby smiles at us, we feel a rush of joy that has us automatically smile back. However, most of our interactions with other people do not have this feeling of connectedness and emotional immediacy. Most of the time we don't even look the people we are addressing in the eye, let alone feel with them. Because of our social training, we tend to regard sharing feelings with other people as threatening. We are taught to close up and defend ourselves, and to keep our interactions as sterile and devoid of feeling as possible.

In order to communicate with plants (or people), you have to be able to regard them as your equals. If you are afraid (ashamed) to talk with homeless people, beggars, crazy people, etc. then you'll also find it difficult to talk with plants. However, it's actually easier to communicate with plants than it is to communicate with people because plants don't have defenses and self-importance agendas in place which engage our own defenses and self-importance agendas. To feel with plants (or people) doesn't mean to gush all over them; all it means is to recognize them as beings whose feelings are as important to them as your feelings are to you. When first learning to communicate with plants, it helps to be in contact with the same individual plants on a daily basis. Ideally you should go out, preferably alone, to the same tree or meadow for at least a few minutes every day. If you can't do this, cultivating garden or house plants will work just as well, although it's easiest to communicate with large trees. This is because from a feeling (light fiber) point of view, humans and trees are very much alike – the light fiber (auric glow) configurations of both humans and trees are quite similar, whereas that of insects, for example, is very different from either. It is easier for humans and trees to communicate with each other than it is for either to communicate with insects.

Now even the least psychic person, going up to a large tree, should be able to pick up something of the personality (mood) of that tree. How does the tree make you feel – happy, sad, loving, jolly, heavy? Can you pick up its sex: sense a male or female presence – or its age: young and vigorous or old and mellow?

This isn't all that hard to do – you can call upon your senses to buttress your feelings, as in the exercise of seeing pictures in the clouds, except that you do it by feeling rather than thinking – by relaxing into the process rather than controlling it. It's exactly what a materialist would term "anthropomorphism."

For example, spiky trees (like palmettos and Joshua trees) have a sassy, masculine energy. Cypress trees tend to be clowns or wise guys. Banana trees are joyous and loving. Weeping trees really do have a doleful air about them. Tall, erect trees have proud and regal personalities. Trees that seem to be reaching longingly for the heavens *are* reaching longingly for the heavens.

A good time to learn to connect emotionally with trees is when they're dying. The next time you see a tree being felled, pause and quiet down your thoughts and watch it attentively. You should easily be able to feel the tree's agony just before it falls, since trees (and all beings) are filled with power at the moment of their deaths and profoundly affect the beings around them. Loggers triumphantly yell "Timber!" when a tree falls to cover their sense of shame and disconnectedness – to block communication with the tree at the moment of its death.

Another good time to pick up on plants' feelings is when they are in motion. Plants are happiest when they are moving – blown by the wind and the rain. Wave back to them when they wave at you (it's only polite). Watch how they dance in the breeze. See how the trees which overhang roads and walkways cast down blessings on all who pass beneath them. See how the young growing tips are more alert, vigorous, and naively impetuous than the older and mellower lower leaves. Be aware of the awareness of plants: when you walk through a wood or meadow, feel as though you were walking through a crowd of people, all of whom are watching you.

Some people pick up on the feelings of plants by seeing faces in the bark or foliage. They impose that thought form (of a face with a giggly, dour, saucy, etc. expression) over the feeling of the tree, since that's how most people are conditioned to interpret feelings – by associating them with facial expressions.

What we're tying to get at are feelings, which can be apprehended directly, without any need for sensory cues. However, the senses can provide a useful point of reference and serve as a bridge between imagination and pure feeling, which is how they function in dreams. When you see with your feelings rather than your mind, your visual attention isn't focused on any one thing, but rather everything within your field of vision strikes your attention with equal impact (vividness), as it does in dreams. To see this way you have to have your mind quiet, and you have to be in a joyous and abandoned mood. If you're bummed out or grumpy, you won't be able to see what plants are feeling any more than you'd be able to see a baby smile at you.

Much of our social training entails learning to stifle our senses – to not see what is right before our eyes, to not listen to what our ears are hearing, to be offended by smells, discomfited by touch. Cutting off our senses leaves us feeling apathetic and disconnected from our world. Therefore, if we want to renew our feeling of connectedness which we had as infants, we have to start plugging our senses into our feelings again. And because they are so nonthreatening, feeling with plants is a good place to start.

Not only do different species of plants have different feelings associated with them, but also there is considerable individual variation in personalities between different plants of the same species, between different branches on the same plant, and even between different leaves on the same branch. By lightly holding a leaf for a moment between your thumb and forefinger, you can feel which leaves want to be picked for medicine or food purposes and which ones want to be left alone. The leaves that want to be picked have a high, vibrant feel to them, whereas leaves that don't want to be picked feel dead in your hand.

Even if you can't seem to tune in to the feelings of plants, you can still telepathically "talk" with them. Plants can talk to you in thoughts, and these (at first) seem indistinguishable from your own thoughts. That is, it will seem to you that you are the one who is thinking these thoughts, when in fact it is the plants which are sending you messages. That's why it's important to have your own mind as quiet as possible – to be in a relaxed mood – if you expect plants to talk to you; if your own mind is buzzing, there's no way the plants can get a word in edgewise. Any thoughts or feelings you have while sitting under a tree or working with plants are probably messages from the plants.

So how do you know if you are actually communicating with a plant, and not just imagining it? The answer is: you don't. You just go with your intuition rather than going with your concepts, what you've been taught. Instead of hypnotizing yourself into believing that the world of concepts is reality, you hypnotize yourself into believing that the world of feelings – of magic – is reality. The only difference between these two equally valid points of view is that from one of them plants talk to you, and from the other they don't. If you feel self-conscious talking to plants, just remember that what you have been programmed to call the "real" world is merely a figment of your imagination also. And if you start calling something else the real world, then that something else becomes the real world; it becomes as real as this one.

If you're dubious, just ask the plant over and over, "Is this you, Mr. or Ms. Plant talking to me, or am I just imagining it?" And if you keep getting the same answer over and over, "It's me, the plant! It's me, the plant!" – then just assume that it is indeed the plant talking to you, and listen to what it has to say. You can ask questions and get answers, both questions and answers coming as though you were holding a conversation in your own mind.

It's easy to learn to talk with house and garden plants, since these are particularly eager to discuss matters such as fertilization, watering, shade, grafting and transplanting techniques, etc. But in addition to such mundane affairs, plants (particularly large trees) can give you helpful advice on all sorts of matters. Take them your problems; ask them what they think you should do. Some of my best friends and most trusted advisors are trees.

Whether you are consciously aware of it or not, you are already communicating with plants all the time. The soothing, healing, tranquilizing feeling that comes when you are gardening or are out in nature is in fact your psychic attunement to the joyous vibrations of the plants around you. To follow this feeling one step further – to its source – is to put yourself into direct communication with the plants. It's as easy as smiling at a baby.

Following Your Feelings

Following feelings is one of the most important psychic techniques, and one of the easiest to learn. It's useful in a pinch – in tight situations which call for split-second decision – and it also shows you how to trust your own abundant inner knowledge.

The practice of following feelings cannot be understood apart from the concept of sensory awareness; i.e., to follow feelings is to switch from conceptual (everyday thinking) awareness to a state of sensory (feeling) awareness. For aficionados of materialistic cognitive philosophy, the distinction being made here is that between operating on conceptual thought forms (aka *memes*, *agents*, or *schema control units*); and operating on sensory thought forms (aka *qualia*). Sensory awareness is not all that different from everyday conceptual, or thinking, awareness, except that it's a bit more vivid and here-and-now, as dreams are. Following feelings is the way in which all animals except humans steer themselves – decide where to go and what to do next.

Following feelings puts you into a state of slightly changed – which I term sensory – awareness. I can tell when I'm in this state because I feel a characteristic buzzing in my head: a sound which is more felt than heard; but it feels different to different people. In this state you are much more sensitive and receptive to feelings – your own, as well as those of other people, spirits, plants, etc. However you are also more vulnerable in this state, and can fall prey to the influence of evil spirits of the night. They can't kill you or anything drastic like that, but they can suck your energy. People are shielded from these entities in their normal, everyday (conceptual) awareness by their dullness and insensitivity (obsessive focus on the necessities of everyday life).

In sensory awareness, your feelings – your intuition, your ability to know something directly – are as operational and functional as is your thinking in conceptual awareness. In conceptual awareness you problem-solve with your thinking, whereas in sensory awareness you do it with your feelings, although you're still able to think, just as in conceptual awareness you're still able to feel. Any time you are feeling feelings in the now moment, you are in sensory awareness. Orgasm, pain, laughter, anger, listening to music, etc. – what some people term "flow" – actually take place in sensory awareness, which interpenetrates conceptual awareness. Sensory awareness is the dream level of everyday life. Any time you are feeling feelings such as pleasure, pain, humor, sadness, hunger, satiety, etc. you are basically dreaming. You are "awake" only when you're thinking. Since thinking and feeling cannot take place at the same time; and since you are thinking most of the time, it seems to you that conceptual (thinking) consciousness is reality, and dreaming (or feeling) consciousness is a kind of nebulous nonsense.

Yet, thinking is a recent invention in human history, not even 12,000 years old. Ancient humans didn't think about what they would do next – they didn't make decisions based on reason – rather they felt what to do next. They just knew what to do, and they did it. This is a more functional mode of operation for a hunter, who has to make a lot of quick decisions in the here-and-now; whereas the thinking mode is more functional for agriculture, trade, etc. where the concern is more for the past and future than for the now. Sensory awareness is closer to ancient humans' perception of the world than is our modern conceptual awareness.

There's not all that great a difference between sensory and conceptual awareness, except that feeling has dominance over thinking. You can still think in sensory awareness, but it's of secondary importance – it takes the back seat, just as feeling takes the back seat in conceptual awareness. Everyone constantly shifts back and forth between the two awarenesses all day every day as they stop thinking momentarily to feel something. The goal is to learn to shift into sensory awareness deliberately – to learn to separate out the two types of awareness and sustain the feeling of feelings beyond the moment, i.e. to be able to move from feeling to feeling in the same way that you move from thought to thought in conceptual awareness. This isn't that hard to do: even the most insensitive schnook should be able to figure out how to enter sensory awareness and follow feelings after a practice session or two.

Each of us has spirit guides who are capable of shifting us into sensory awareness, i.e., teaching us how to follow our feelings. In fact, this is their main function. They try to do this to us all the time, but most of us are too busy thinking – clinging to conceptual awareness – to pay attention to them. Even if you are not able to consciously channel your spirit guides e.g. by automatic writing, rest assured that they are quite capable of shifting your awareness for you just the same. If you make a firm decision to learn to follow your feelings in good faith, they'll pick up the ball and do the rest. Trust them. If you follow these instructions, your guides will lead you unerringly.

In the beginning, while you're still learning the technique, it's not actually your own feelings that you are following, but rather your spirit guides' feelings. You temporarily relinquish your feelings to them, and they direct things and decide for you where you'll go next. Your guides will send you loud and clear messages that even little old unpsychic you will be able to read. Later, as you understand what you're about, they'll hand the reins back to you, and from then on you're on your own.

From then on the job of becoming a magician entails losing your self-importance (self-pity). Self-importance and following feelings work inversely: as one goes down, the other goes up: as focus (the obsession of everyday, thinking awareness) is decreased, awareness increases. Focus is the opposite of awareness. Sensory awareness is like a Disney animation, when the young maiden enters the forest and all the flowers and trees and butterflies and animals come alive and sing and dance around her in welcome. Follow these instructions, and that's kind of like what happens.

To begin to follow your feelings, go out alone to a place in nature away from people. You *can* go with someone else, but the tendency then is to try to slough the responsibility off onto the other person. You're going to die alone, so you might as well try to learn to live alone. It's best to do this at night at first, while you're still learning the technique, after you've already had a few hours' sleep. Once you master the technique, however, you can make the shift in awareness yourself any time, day or night. But the learning should be done at night because feelings are stronger at night. That is why we're afraid of the dark in conceptual awareness – it symbolizes feeling. In the state of sensory awareness the night isn't scary, but invigorating.

Take off all your clothes. If there's very rough ground or a real danger of cutting your feet, you may leave your shoes on; otherwise, go barefoot. The reason you go naked is to more easily feel the forces around you – the earth, wind, etc. – which are dulled by clothing. Also, if there's any chance of your being discovered, going naked helps to keep you alert. If it's cold or rainy, so much the better. Comfort is the enemy of feeling. To feel the world, you have to be raw and naked and vulnerable.

There is less sense of past and future in sensory awareness – most of the attention is attuned to the now moment. The past must be dropped to enter into sensory awareness; everything takes off from right this moment. This is another reason to take off your clothes: it symbolizes taking off your personal history. You needn't have your mind in a state of complete quiescence, but you shouldn't be all worried and buzzing, either. You should be alert, relaxed, and expectant.

Face east. It is helpful to be able to read the cardinal directions from the stars; but if you can't do this, or if it's cloudy, wear a compass around your neck. At all times and places you should always know where the cardinal directions lie. Now, see if you can feel a "pull" or "tug" in one direction. If not, turn slowly to your right until you feel a pull in one direction. You can use your eyes to help out: scan the area in front of you as you turn, to see if some one direction "looks" right. It's difficult to explain what this pull is supposed to feel or look like; if you just go out there and try it, you'll find that doing it is a lot easier than thinking about it or trying to describe it. Once you've done it once or twice, you'll have the idea; there's nothing abstruse about it whatsoever. In fact, we've all operated in sensory awareness when we were babies, so it's not as if we're conjuring up an alien state of consciousness from scratch.

If you feel silly out there in the wilderness in the middle of the night; or if you feel bemused or fretful about what you're supposed to be doing; know that this is just your self-importance (self-pity) trying to assert itself by copping out of taking responsibility for being here now. Following feelings must be done by feeling, not thinking. Wondering "Am I doing this right?" is an absurd (albeit natural) question – absurd, because the very asking of it is "wrong". Such a question makes sense in conceptual awareness because there feelings don't matter much – the important thing is the impression you're making on other people. In conceptual awareness the question "Am I doing this right?" is not only sensible, it is the very crux. But in sensory awareness you are following your own feelings, so there's no way to refer judgments to anyone else – no one but you can feel your feelings.

Now if you feel fearful, that's okay. It's normal for people to feel fearful when their self-importance is under attack. Take a few deep breaths, sit down, and relax. Look around; listen to the sounds; feel the night.

Because following feelings bypasses the thinking level, there's really no way to block it – you can't help but succeed. To be running around naked in the wilderness in the middle of the night is to be in sensory awareness. If you're out there at all, you're doing it right.

Now, when you feel that one direction is the "right" one, start walking in that direction. Take care not to have any preconceived ideas, because things can change at any moment. If a moment before you felt that you should go a certain way, but now you feel you should go a different way, by all means drop the earlier idea and go with how you feel now. You can't flip on an automatic pilot in sensory awareness – that just flips you back into conceptual awareness. You have to be constantly alert to the feeling of what direction you should be going in. In the beginning, when your spirit guides are still directing you, they'll likely throw some direction changes in there at random to keep you on the *qui vive*. If you're in doubt, just face east again and start over. If two different directions seem to pull you, switch from one to the other – scan one and then the other – to see which one feels "stronger".

If all else fails, spin around in a clockwise direction faster and faster until you get dizzy and collapse on the ground. Whatever direction you are facing (or your head is pointing) when you fall is the direction you should go in.

Following feelings means following feelings. Fear of being lost is not a feeling; it's thinking. You can only be lost in the future, because in the now moment you're always right there, where you're standing. So if you indulge in worrying about whether you're getting lost, you've shifted out of sensory awareness and are back in conceptual awareness. In sensory awareness you know that by relaxing and following your feelings you'll always arrive at the place where you're supposed to be. If you don't have this conviction – this calm certainty – then you've shifted out of sensory awareness.

So get a grip on yourself! Don't stand there pretending that you don't understand. In conceptual awareness you can pretend you don't know what's happening, you can get away with playing dumb; in fact, in conceptual awareness, that's what's expected. But sensory awareness means taking responsibility for your decisions instead of wringing your hands helplessly and pretending you don't know what's what.

Whenever you feel as though you've gotten off the track or have lost the thread, you get back on the track by starting from right where you are, and following your feelings from there. Face east, etc., or spin around until you get dizzy and fall.

When following feelings at night you must keep especially alert to smells, since these can help guide you as much in the dark as sight does in the daytime. There are smells that indicate danger, others that mean protection, happiness, etc. You pick up this kind of information as you go along, without really having to think about it.

In general, you should avoid depressions (low spots) in the land since they're energy depleting. You can feel how depressions have low vibrations: sounds become lower, like a pressure in your ears or head; or you feel as though you are walking through something viscous. On a "high" way things are cleaner and clearer: you are more alert and joyous. In a depression your tendency is to walk slumped over, with your head down; whereas on a high way you walk erect, head up, chest out, happier.

One exercise your spirit guides may have you do is to jump from precipices or into bodies of water, etc. on command. This is to teach you abandon, split-second decision, acting without thinking or hesitating, as babies do when they reach out to grasp something with no fear that this is going to send them crashing to the floor. It is necessary to learn (or relearn) this abandon because there are times in life when abandon is required – when there is no time for shilly-shallying or fiddling around with indecision. It is natural to be hesitant at first, especially since spirit guides don't seem to care how much something's going to hurt. But after a while you get to a point where you can jump on command without a second thought or any fear of injury (of course, you get injured a lot while learning this lesson)

Now, just as our spirit guides are able to do, there are beings of the night which can imitate our own feelings when we are in sensory awareness, which we are protected from in conceptual awareness by our sheer insensitivity. These beings can imitate your sense of direction to lure you to them so they can tap into and suck your energy – make you sick or depressed for a few days after your encounter with them. It's easiest to avoid these entities by leading a strong, disciplined life; that way they can't sway you so easily. But the way you can tell the difference between your own feelings and the pull of an evil spirit is that the evil spirit's "call" has a faint sense of urgency or intranquility behind it, which your own feelings never have. Just remember this: if you are ever in a situation where one part of you wants to venture forward and another part wants to get the hell out of there, follow the latter impulse. This business of evil spirits is not meant to daunt the tyro, but rather to map out the terrain as completely as possible. It's all part and parcel of learning to trust your own feelings. You'll run into the little suckers here and there, and they'll zap you and make you ill for a few days, but it's no biggie. The only way to learn how to avoid them is by blowing it a few times.

When following feelings in the presence of other people, pay very close attention to everything they say and do. Anything that someone offers you when you are following your feelings should be regarded as a true gift of power – a power object. If you are offered food, you should regard it as power food and eat it slowly, mindfully, and gratefully. Any objects (e.g. leaves, stones, feathers) which call your attention and "ask" you to take them should be picked up and regarded as power objects. Only by being strong and following your heart can you know what to pick up and what to avoid. The whole thing happens instantaneously.

As a tool, the technique of following feelings is useful in locating power spots and the abodes of nature spirits. But beyond that, it's often helpful in everyday situations. I was once in a group of tourists in a resort town, and we were all hungry but couldn't decide where to eat. One person wanted to go to one restaurant, but the others didn't like that place. It was Monday night, and all the restaurants that we could agree on were closed. And one person wanted pizza, another felt like yogurt with fruit, and another wanted fried chicken.

We were walking past closed restaurant after closed restaurant, debating what to do and getting nowhere, when I got an impulse to follow my feelings. "Follow me!" I said optimistically. My feelings led us away from the tourist section of town, up towards where the natives lived. I knew that there were no more restaurants up that way, but I soldiered on, growing more dubious all the time. Finally we came across a restaurant I'd never noticed before, probably because it had never been open any time I'd passed that way before. We went in, and they had pizza, and yogurt with fruit, and fried chicken. The food was delicious and the place was friendly and enjoyable.

But the significance of this technique goes beyond its mundane utility. When you learn to follow your feelings, you know that your feelings will always be there, and you can rely on them. You don't have to worry about how you will handle the future; you don't need insurance and social security and hedges against the future; because you know that no matter what happens, you'll always be able to follow your feelings. The practice of following feelings teaches you trust – trust in your own feelings, trust in the situation in which you find yourself, and trust that you will be able to deal with whatever might happen.

Water Spirits

Self-transformation is an enigmatic process; we all know what we *ought* to be like, how we *ought* to be thinking and acting, but we don't know how to actually do it. Even when we can look back on ways in which we have grown spiritually over the years, we can't really understand how we got from there to here. In other words, self-transformation is a process which we can never understand intellectually, but can only feel.

In fact, the essence of self-transformation is a lessening of our sense of importance. The theory of importance is discussed at great length in my book *Thought Forms*; in essence, importance is like a "glue" that we use to hold ourselves together, or a shield we put up against our deaths. Without it we would be in the same position as a newborn – completely passive, vulnerable, and incapable of accomplishing anything. Our sense of separatedness – our feeling that there is an "I" there – is ultimately a product of our importance.

On the other hand, importance is also the cause of our suffering: a barrier that not only keeps our deaths at bay, but which also separates us from and closes our hearts to other people, and our own true feelings. To erase our importance is to feel the barriers which separate us from other people lessening, but also to open ourselves up to the feeling of death breathing down our necks.

There are many techniques used for erasing importance. The one I have found to be most effective, easy, and joyous is going to nature spirits, particularly tree and water spirits. While some nature spirits, such as mountain and cave spirits, can be rather strict and tricky to deal with or require a lot of propitiation, tree and water spirits are gentle and mellow (the ocean and her attendant undines can be rather nasty at times, and these spirits should be approached with the greatest respect. The assumption in this essay is that you will be using spirits of inland waterways.).

Go out alone to a river or creek in an undeveloped area where there aren't any people. You should go alone because if you go with a friend you will tend to keep referring your judgments back to the friend for validation instead of taking responsibility for your intuitive judgments yourself. When you don't know what you're doing, it's always better to do it alone.

Start walking upstream, paying close attention to the sights and sounds. Water spirits tend to be at places where there are springs, bends in the river, deep pools, cataracts, rapids, etc. Usually there are also striking physical features at such places – unusual vegetation on the banks, or interesting rock formations. There's often a distinct change in the sound the river makes – if it's been gurgling, it suddenly becomes calm, or the reverse. In other words, there are usually sensory clues to indicate that a water spirit is indeed present. However you should also be able to *feel* that there's a water spirit there – that this particular place along the river has a unique feeling (personality) to it. Whenever you get the feeling that you've arrived at the right place, rest assured that you've arrived at the right place. Trust yourself.

Sit down on the bank and relax. Talk to the spirit. You won't feel silly doing this if you're alone. Tell the spirit who you are and why you've come. Ask it to help you wash away your importance. Then take off your clothes and jump in, or if it's shallow, just splash around. Don't use soap. If the water is unpolluted, take a little sip. Then thank the spirit, dry off, and leave.

You should go back to this spirit every single day, if possible, and repeat the exercise. If you can't do it every day, then go as often as you can, though that should be at least once a week, even if this means in the snow. You should also go anytime someone has dumped a heavy bad vibe on you, or you feel depressed, desperate, or self-pitying. You may not feel much difference after your first visits to the water spirit, but after a while you will definitely feel what that spirit is doing to you. There will be times – especially when you go to the spirit in a mood of great turmoil and upset – when you will be amazed by how much the spirit can calm you and soothe you.

Water spirits actually "eat" your importance – to them it's a kind of food you are offering them, so the relationship is symbiotic, it's not as if you are the only one benefiting. However, it's a good idea to take the spirit a little present occasionally, such as a bunch of flowers, a pretty stone, or some food items you have made lovingly yourself (a token portion will suffice). One wouldn't suppose that spirits would care about such things, but in fact they are delighted with little presents and the thoughtfulness behind them.

You can get holy water from the water spirit, to be used for blessing, purifying, etc. You should do this on the dark of the moon, with the moon waning and before it has risen, with the moon in a water sign (Cancer, Scorpio or Pisces). Ask the spirit to bless the water for you as you draw it.

As you get to know your spirit better you'll acquire a great fondness for it, and come to regard your visits to it as the high point of your day or week. After a couple of months you will find your everyday life becoming calmer, more peaceful and relaxed, without any obvious reason for it.

Why Love Relationships Fail

Love relationships fail because at no time in our training by society are we given a factual model of what a love relationship is, or are told how to make one succeed. There are fundamentally three levels on which intimate relationships operate, and our social training only prepares us to deal with one of them – the most superficial one – and even that one ineptly. This superficial level is called the *expectations level*. It is usually the only level we address consciously.

The expectations level consists of all our self-images and self-importance. When we primp ourselves in front of a mirror, what we are primping is our expectations of other people. It's the level of our daydreams and fantasies, whereon everyone is as impressed with us as we are with ourselves.

On the expectations level what interests us the most about a prospective partner is his or her physical attractiveness, manner of dress and bearing, social and educational background, future prospects, how "cool" he or she is, how he or she reflects back on us, what others will think of us for having chosen this partner.

On the expectations level a "love relationship" is actually an approval agreement, a contract, To Wit: "The party of the first part hereby agrees to pretend to honor, love, cherish and obey the party of the second part; in return for which considerations the party of the second part agrees not to hurt, betray, nor expose to public embarrassment the party of the first part (see appended schedule of specific acts which shall be deemed to constitute 'hurt', 'betrayal', and 'public embarrassment'). Any violation of this agreement by either party shall be considered valid grounds for spitefulness, vengeance, and all manner of carrying on like a big baby."

On the expectations level we submit ourselves to another person not for love, but for approval. Love and approval have nothing to do with one another. Love is a light, joyous, happy feeling; receiving approval is a tight, clinging, possessive feeling, which does, however, have an ego rush behind it. That ego rush is not joy – it's glory, self-importance, which we have been trained to seek instead of love.

The expectations level must eventually wear out because its basic premise is getting something for nothing. On this level everything we're putting out ("giving") is phony – it's just to impress other people, or to get something more in return. We're putting out phoniness in the hope of getting something real (happiness) back. And that's not how the universe is set up. There are no free lunches or free rides out there.

What fools us is that most of the messages we receive – from our parents and peers, our teachers and preachers, our leaders and the media – are that the expectations level works; and if it doesn't, that's our fault and we should be ashamed of ourselves.

For whom is it working? Look around. How many truly happy marriages are you aware of (of more than ten years' duration, since it can take that long or longer for the expectations level to wear thin). Sure, there are some, but not many; and usually the people involved in truly happy marriages are very, very special people in their own right.

Isn't this true? But there are also lots of relationships which appear to be happy on the surface, but are actually miserable underneath: both partners have learned to repress their true feelings and resign themselves to unhappiness without showing it. These people never get beyond the expectations level.

The reason why the expectations level inevitably crashes – although it *can* and often *does* mellow into true love after the crash – is because it is wholly narcissistic: it doesn't include the other person. It does not permit the other person to *be* a person, but only a reflection of our own fondest self-images. It doesn't allow the other person space to be real – to have feelings of his or her own.

For example, is our partner permitted to have sex with whomever he / she wishes? Is our partner even permitted to be sexually turned on by anyone but us? Is our partner permitted to tell us that we are not a satisfying lover? The list could go on and on. Only sexual expectations are mentioned here because those are practically universal, but we have all sorts of other fences we try to erect around our partners to keep them pristine and unsullied for us – expectations that they will agree with us about money, child raising, career, religion, etc.; expectations that they will forego making their own decisions in order to support us.

The expectations level must eventually crash under its own weight by sheer exhaustion. When people are involved with one another in an approval agreement, or any agenda that is not love, then everyone has to work overtime in order to convince the other or to convince oneself; and this is painful to bear.

In every relationship there is a power equation: someone has more control than the other person. The power in a relationship at any given moment resides in the hands of that one of the partners who has the least stake in the continuance of the relationship. Typically, therefore, the power equation in a relationship will teeter-totter back and forth over time (and over different lifetimes) – now this person, now that one, being the one presently calling the shots. The only way to undo this little tango is to undo all expectations.

The expectations level would be problematical and contradictory enough if it were the only level on which we relate with other people. Unfortunately, there are two deeper levels which actually govern the course of our relationships, and these deeper levels contradict the expectations level.

The level which underlies and controls the expectations level, which assures that the expectations level will eventually crash, or be maintained in great suffering, is the *conditioning level*. It's the level of our basic conditioning by society, which is to hate ourselves. Beneath the glitter and glory of our expectations, our self-images, is the grim truth that we are actually ashamed of ourselves. We are taught to be dissatisfied with ourselves by our parents and society.

Whereas the expectations level is set up so that people will be "nice" to each other (make the agreement: "I won't expose you as a liar and phony if you won't expose me as a liar and phony"), the conditioning level is set up to divide people, to make them fear and distrust each other. We are not trained to relate intimately with one another, but rather to wage war upon one another – to feel hurt, jealous, competitive, critical; to pick at each other and bend each other out of shape – rather than to be happy and accepting. The parent / child relationship is the basic war setup; the man / woman war is grafted on top.

While on an expectations level we tell ourselves that what we want is to live happily ever after, we are conditioned by our society to hate ourselves and to deny ourselves the very love which we consciously tell ourselves that we are seeking. We are trained by our parents to hate ourselves in precisely the same fashion in which our parents hated themselves.

The conditioning level is the level which psychotherapy addresses (unfortunately, after the damage is already done). We are so overwhelmed by our parents when we are little – so awed by their divinity – that we are afraid to express, or allow ourselves to feel openly, anger at them, or any other feeling of which they would not approve – which contradicts *their* expectations. Thus our parents' expectations level becomes our conditioning level.

Society calls infatuation with our own self-images "love"; and so on an expectations level we tell ourselves that we are going into relationships to get "love"; whereas on a conditioning level we are going into relationships to deny ourselves love – to pinpoint, through the mirroring of another person, precisely how we ourselves are incapable of giving and receiving love.

One might well wonder why people would want to reenact the situations out of their childhood which brought them the most pain and trauma. The reason is that those wounds never healed properly. They are still raw and suppurating, and extremely tender to the touch. Only by tearing those wounds back open again and cleaning out all the dreck, the self-hatred, can a true healing occur. And only by staging a situation similar to the one which produced those wounds originally can the wounds be reopened (actually this isn't the only way of doing it; there are far more skillful ways of doing it, such as active imagination. However, this is the most popular way of doing it).

Just as on the expectations level our goal is the validation of our images, on the conditioning level our goal is to recreate all the emotional turmoil our parents inflicted on us, but this time around to grab the brass ring of love which our parents denied us.

Up until recently society has had the fifth Commandment and a raft of social sanctions in place against examining the conditioning level too closely. Freud was one of the first to take a good, hard look at this level of human interaction. And at the present time there are lots of good popular books available on the subject of toxic parents, how we all marry our father or mother, and seek in marriage the precise same hurt and nonfulfillment which our principle caregivers made us feel in infancy. The problem is that we don't bother reading these books until our relationships are already in deep trouble. These books should be required reading for all high school students.

"Don't blame your parents! Just wait until you're a parent yourself!" they (our parents) tell us. Well, that's wrong; we should blame our parents, because only by consciously blaming them are we in a position to consciously forgive them. Only when we can see that it was their own self-hatred which their parents laid on them that impelled them to do what they did to us; only when we can see them as people in as much or more pain as we, who really did try to do the best for us they knew how; only then can we forgive our parents. And only then can we forgive ourselves, and let go of our own self-hatred, no longer needing to reenact it or to blame ourselves over and over because we loved our parents, and all they cared about was being right.

The third (and deepest) level of relationship is the *karma level* – the level of the lessons we are trying to learn from certain people, based upon our experiences with them in other lifetimes and realities. Anything which is wrong or out-of-kilter in a relationship originates on the karma level. Our gut-level, first impressions of people are often good indicators of the kind of karma we have going with them; but our conscious minds often bury such information directly as it is perceived.

For example, it could happen that the reason we are sexually turned on by a certain person is that in a previous life we raped and tortured that person; for some aeons, perhaps, that individual has been itching for a lifetime in which to right matters. That might be the karma we have set up with someone; but all our conscious mind knows, on its level of expectation, is that we are sexually turned on by that person and want the person to validate it by having sex with us. And so we put our head in that person's noose, and wonder later on why things aren't working out as we'd imagined.

The karma and conditioning levels work in tandem to control the actual circumstances and course of a relationship. For example, if on the conditioning level we decide to reenact a parent's abandonment of us and we choose a partner who will abandon us, we might select for that role someone whom in a previous lifetime we abandoned. This can be considered a penance; but we can also look at it as a kind of "you scratch my back and I'll scratch yours" – like saying, "I made you suffer in that lifetime, and now I want to know how you felt – to feel the feelings I made you feel." On the karma level, as on the conditioning level, we try to restage events which will produce a resonance with some unresolved emotional issue in the totality of our being.

The agendas we have set up with other people on the karma level are often revealed in the very first impressions we have of them and which we immediately repress. It's hard to describe this, and it's different for everyone, but often upon meeting someone with whom we have a heavy karmic agenda going, we get a FLASH, a conscious feeling or thought, of something we desire or feel threatened by about that person. And then we immediately "forget" what we just felt, because if we have bad karma going with the person, then that flash was of a side of ourselves which we don't want to consciously face or acknowledge – a side we are calling upon that person to enact openly for us, to ram down our throat for us, until we're forced to acknowledge it. Thus we "forget" this first impression, and later on pretend we don't understand why the person we loved and trusted so much could have changed so.

Of course, we can run past-life regressions to check what sort of karma we have going with someone before getting seriously involved with them – sort of like running a credit or AIDS check on a prospective spouse. In India astrology has been historically relied upon for this sort of information. But we can also avoid difficulties just by being alert to our own gut feelings and intuitive impressions of other people, rather than ignoring this most essential information in a relationship.

Thus the basic intensity or emotional theme of a relationship is set up on the karma level; the particular script, the sequence of events which will unfold in a relationship, is set up on the conditioning level; and the costuming, the superficial appearances or show put on for the benefit of the neighbors, is set up on the expectations level.

The glare of the expectations level blinds us to what is happening on the two deeper levels; and the expectations level is a lie. What is actually going on in a relationship on the conditioning and karma levels is always quite visible; but we pretend we don't see it, we pretend we don't understand it, in order to uphold our expectations as long as possible.

By "lie" is meant something that we feel, but which we suppress or conceal. For example, if our sex partner is doing something that doesn't feel good and turns us off, and we lay there and take it because we're too embarrassed to speak up and possibly hurt our partner's feelings, then that's a lie. Any time we do not communicate something we are feeling because we are embarrassed to do so, or because we don't want to hurt or provoke the other person or become a target for his or her disapproval, we are lying. Lying leads to sneaking around behind the other person's back. Lies lead to more lies.

We can tell if lying is taking place in a relationship this way: if there is an area in which we don't trust the other person; where we withhold from the other person; where we are afraid of the other person (his / her disapproval or rejection); where we feel something other than GOOD about the person; then that is a place where we are lying. We are trained to lie to other people, and then to feel betrayed when our lies are exposed.

All a lie is, is a contradiction. Lies must always exist in pairs, whereas the truth – love – just is. For example, on the level of our expectations we might set up the pair: "I want you to be honest with me" and "I don't want to hear how turned on you are by someone else." On the level of our conditioning we might set up the pair: "I truly love you, mommy!" and "I'll never question your love for me!" On the level of karma lies don't exist per se (it's repressing this level that makes a lie out of it); but one could say that the basic lie or duality of the karma level is: "You and I are two" and "You and I are one."

All the lies in a relationship are laid down right at the beginning. By "laid down" is meant: conscious. Conscious for a moment, and then – just as consciously – repressed, ignored, "forgotten". The basic lies of the karma level may be laid down in the first few seconds of a relationship. The lies of the conditioning level (the game plan of who's going to hurt whom, and how) are usually laid down at the time the relationship is formalized – when the mutual decision is made to commit, to get serious as it were. And the expectations level is a complete lie from the first pop.

Anyone with their eyes open could see what's going on. Sometimes our parents, friends, or other people who care about us try to pass us warnings. But we're "so much in love" and "love is blind" and we're so "happy" that we don't want to see it. We don't want anything to call us down from this lovely cloud we're on; this lovely lie we're telling ourselves.

And for each and every lie, the piper must be paid. There's a karmic law at work in all this, and EVERY single lie, no matter how teensy-weensy, will someday have to be brought into the open and admitted, else the relationship is doomed – doomed to be something other than a love relationship, because in a love relationship there is no room whatsoever for lies of any kind, at any time, for any reason.

All the alarm about the soaring divorce rate in our society, the call for a return to "traditional values", is a bunch of baloney. Those traditional values were a total lie, and it's amazing that the human race put up with that lie as long as it did. Traditional values means you get married on the expectations level and you never question it. You learn somehow to live with a lie, with unhappiness, and you bite your tongue because the social sanctions (what the neighbors might think) against divorce were so stringent. Instead of returning to living out lies, our society ought to stop glorifying the expectations level. As is the case also with war, when society stops glorifying infatuation people will stop seeking it.

Love relationships fail because we go into them with a lot of la-de-da thought forms about who we are and what we expect to get, and we run smack into heavy karma and conditioning agendas we had no conscious idea even existed. We are not consciously aware of what expectations we have until those expectations aren't fulfilled; and we don't understand what our parents did to us until we find our partner doing the same thing – make us feel that old, familiar feeling in the pit of our stomach.

As long as we're relating to the other person on one of these three levels, we're not relating to an actual person at all, but only to our own self-reflection, our childhood wounds, or our deep-seated fears and insecurities. On the expectations level our attention is focused on the future; on the conditioning level it's focused on the past; and on the karma level it's focused on the remote past. A true love relationship, however, involves relating to a real, live person in the now moment.

Earth Magic

The salient feature of magical training is learning to use the world around us for validation, rather than the devices of people; to come to appreciate more the gurgling of water in a stream, the whisper of the wind in our ears, and the healing warmth of a tree, rather than the approval of people. All of our unhappiness in life stems from our trying to live up to the expectations of people, and our having forgotten what ancient humans knew: that we are first and foremost children of the earth, and that she loves us from the bottom of her heart.

The earth isn't insensible, as we've been led to believe. She is vibrantly alive. She can heal us, soothe us, and provide us with a sense of complete and unconditional acceptance. She can nurture and protect us even more than our human mothers – being human – could possibly do. We don't have to feel at odds with the world, like alien interlopers in a hostile environment. The earth is just busting to cuddle us with her love, if we would only make an effort to reach out to her.

We do this simply by 1) acknowledging that she is alive, sentient, and capable of communicating with us; and 2) acknowledging daily our debt to her and thanking her for all her gifts. Try doing the following earth ritual every day: dawn or sunset are the best times, but do it whenever you conveniently can. Go out to a place in nature (if possible), take off all your clothes (if possible), and prostrate yourself face down with arms outstretched above your head pointing in the direction of the sun. Begin to breathe out (exhale hard) all your angry, frustrated, depressed, negative feelings into the earth to be buried, and inhale the healing, soothing energy of the earth. Feel it fill your body with warmth on the inbreaths as the negative energy dissipates on the outbreaths. Then, when you are calm, kiss the earth and thank her, knowing that from the earth you have come, and to the earth you shall return.

Even if you don't feel anything out of the ordinary while doing this exercise, keep plugging away at it, and at some point you will realize that the earth is "talking" to you. Some naturally talented people pick up the thread the first time out; however, most people have to do it on faith for a while until the establish a clear telepathic / intuitive communications link with the earth. At that point the earth herself will give you instructions and tell you what to do; you'll just "know" it. For example, one thing she might have you do is to gaze at her. This is accomplished by slightly crossing your eyes but keeping them relaxed; calming down your thoughts; and staring without focusing at whatever feature in your field of vision most attracts your attention. The earth can give you all sorts of information in this way. If you do the earth ritual at dawn, try gazing at the vapors which rise from the earth in the early morning, since these are full of messages.

Everybody's experiences with the earth ritual are different, so about all that can definitively be said on the subject is, be prepared for some surprises! If you carry this ritual out in good faith and with the expectation of ultimate success, then in a few weeks or months you'll get it working as described. The only trick to making magic work is patience – long continuance of the same ritual act (repetition of the same desire).

Another ritual which can be used in conjunction with or apart from the daily earth ritual is the burial ritual. You use this one whenever you are especially burdened, ill, careworn, or depressed. The earth has an infinite capacity not only to heal but also to absorb and dissipate negative energy, and every sort of spiritual and emotional heaviness as well as chronic illness.

It helps to fast the day before this ritual. Dig a trench two feet deep and somewhat longer than your body. Line the trench with sawdust or leaves so you will have a soft bed and pillow to lie on, and make sure your face will be shaded from the sun. Disrobe and wrap yourself in a sheet with only your face exposed (the sheet serves as a protection against e.g. ants). You can smear insect repellant on your face, neck, and hair to keep bugs away. Then lie down in the trench, get comfortable, and have someone cover you with a layer of earth up to your neck with your head sticking out. Have someone visit you every hour or two in case you need a drink and to make sure you're okay. If you have to pee, just do it.

If you are very sick or in desperate need of lightening up, you should remain buried for 12 hours (dawn to dusk) the first time you bury yourself, and for at least 6 hours on subsequent burials (8 is better). Average people only need four hour burials to tune themselves (there's not much point in doing it for less than four hours at a stretch). How long and how frequently you bury yourself depend on how sick or heavy you were to begin with: you come to "know" when it's time to bury yourself again.

Although this ritual may seem to be an odd thing to do, you might just find that being buried is one of the most enjoyable experiences you've ever had. The earth herself is your hostess, and she will do her best to comfort, nourish, and entertain you.

Another way of making intimate contact with the earth is to walk around barefoot as much as possible. If you live in a place where you can't walk around barefoot, maybe it would be worthwhile to move to a place where you can – it is *that* important. Wearing shoes cuts off most of the healing energy and sense of rootedness which the earth would otherwise give us through our feet.

These rituals aren't immutable – you can alter them at will to suit your own taste and convenience. What is important is your seriousness of purpose, the strength of your desire to communicate with the earth, and your willingness to pursue this intent in a deliberate fashion – to make it one of the high priorities in your life. Then your success is assured: you will find a true sense of worth and belonging in the world which doesn't depend on what other people think of you.

Luck

Luck is not a subjective state, but rather is a force out there in the world at large. As is the case also with vitality and physical strength, some people are just born with lots of luck (make the choice to be lucky in this incarnation), whereas others are born with very little luck. However, there are things we can do to increase our luck, since ultimately luck – albeit an outside force – is controlled by our attitude.

Luck has nothing to do with morality, or how nice we are. If a selfish, nasty, manipulative S.O.B. believes that he is lucky, he'll *be* lucky. It's the belief that we are lucky that makes us lucky, not how virtuous we are. If we expect luck to happen, it will tend to happen; whereas if we expect failure, that's what we'll get. People who tend to be lucky also tend to expect luck to happen; and the reverse. So the state of being lucky or unlucky tends to perpetuate itself.

Luck is not the same thing as getting what we think we want. How often has it happened that there was something that we desperately wanted; and we didn't get it and were disappointed; and later on we discovered that it was a darn good thing we didn't get it – it was lucky we didn't get it – because if we had gotten it we would have been sorry, or else we wouldn't have gotten this better thing instead; but at the time of our disappointment we considered ourselves unlucky.

What luck is, is the sense that the world is sustaining, protecting, and nourishing us. It's the feeling that we are being taken care of and provided for, that the impersonal forces of the universe are watching out for us and helping us. Although luck is not the same thing as getting what we think we want, it nonetheless leads to it: getting what we want is a byproduct of the attitude that we are being helped and cared for; that we are deserving and worthy of happiness.

Luck is not the same thing as happiness. Luck is like income, and happiness is like assets. We *do* need some luck to accumulate happiness; but just luck by itself is valueless. If we take our luck for granted, if we "spend" our luck as fast as it comes along (by seeking things which won't ultimately lead us to happiness), then luck will lead us to disaster. Luck is the ability to make things happen for ourselves. If luck is not used to seek love, then no matter how many of the things we want we actually get, we'll tend to become unhappier and unhappier as we go along. Luck (getting what we want) without wisdom (knowing what we truly want in our heart of hearts) inevitably leads to destruction.

Luck, then, can be a force for the negative as well as for the positive. If life tends to hand us pretty much everything we want with little pother on our parts, then we become lazy, indulgent, and unfeeling. As Nero Wolfe put it, we are all much vainer of our luck than of our merits. When we are lucky we tend to believe that God is on our side; that we are above the common lot of mankind. We tend to sneer at other people's bad luck; curl in on ourselves; become smug and complacent – and also shamelessly indifferent to the feelings of others. Thus we cut ourselves off from love with a cozy self-stroking.

In a sense, people who are lucky *do* have a basis for their contempt for unlucky people, since luck is – after all – a disciplined state of mind, an unwavering faith in oneself. Unlucky people tend to be wimpy and invite contempt through their irresponsibility (whining in self-pity as opposed to seizing the reins of control over their lives). However most lucky people have little of the "there but for the grace of God go I" attitude. They tend to forget that they are lucky because they were born with luck – they didn't do anything in this lifetime to earn it. They easily come to believe that they *deserve* their good fortune. Luck may be defined as the absence of doubt; if absence of doubt combines with absence of altruism (dedication to some abstract ideal over and above self-gratification), then luck will lead to an increasingly narrow and selfish focus. Thus luck is as much the road to hell as it is the road to heaven.

Luck operates as quick little flashes every now and again. Lucky people (those with a lucky attitude) are attuned to their lucky chances when they occur. They have the patience to wait before acting until the moment is ripe; and then, when a lucky chance pops up, they see it and grab it. Conversely, when a lucky chance pops up before unlucky people, they reject it automatically. They don't see or understand that that opportunity was their lucky chance, so either they don't notice it at all, or else they notice it but reject it.

Thus there's the same amount of luck going on for everybody all the time, but lucky people, by their attitude, are positioned to make use of it, whereas unlucky people aren't. They are too hung up in their own preconceived expectations of what they think they want; they're like spoiled children trying to order the Spirit around. Instead of receiving gratefully what the Spirit chooses to give them, they angrily reject the Spirit's gifts because they don't conform to their precise images of what they think they want.

Luck and doubt work inversely – each one serves to vanquish the other. The absence of doubt is responsible for the phenomenon known as "beginner's luck". Beginners don't have doubts about what they are doing – it looks easy, so they try it and find that it *is* easy. They don't know enough to grasp all the pitfalls and complexities in what they are doing instinctively (by intuition).

Therefore, to increase luck, it is necessary to banish doubt. The hard part is, that just as it takes money to make money, it takes luck to believe that we are lucky. That's what makes it so hard to break out of a bad luck streak. The reason why people get into bad luck streaks in the first place is because our society encourages doubt, not luck. Society wants people to believe that their best chance for luck is to play the game by society's rules, rather than to follow their own dreams and feelings and hunches. Those who try to strike on their own are met with great resistance and doubt by their fellows: by banks, government and business institutions, their own family and friends. Therefore, a truly lucky attitude also requires being close-mouthed about oneself and one's affairs, so as not to become a target for other people's jealousy, which is the same thing as their doubt, which they can hurl to arouse one's own doubt.

What unlucky people are really striving for – which unlucky people must learn to see within themselves if they are to change their luck – is self-pity. And unlucky people get it. They are as lucky at getting what they want (excuses to pity themselves) as lucky people are at getting what *they* want. Self-pity is a drain on the energy needed to bring luck. We each have only a finite amount of energy, which we can spend on either luck or self-pity, but not both. It is our society which teaches us to pity ourselves – which stands to gain from our collective self-pity and "helplessness".

Changing from an unlucky to a lucky attitude is hard to do – no bones about it. To arbitrarily adopt an attitude of carefree abundance when we're flat broke and being pressed by creditors, or an attitude of radiant good health when we're dying of AIDS, isn't easy to do. The only motivation we have is that there is no choice – it's either change, or self-pity. It's a true triumph of the will to be able to arrive at an attitude of being nourished and protected even though *nothing* is going right. True luck is being able to maintain our equanimity, our cool, our belief that we're in good shape, even in the midst of a maelstrom.

So now we come down to the question of how we can change our luck. Astrology (propitious times to act or not act), charms, talismans, etc. can help us to focus our energy on our intent to become lucky. They work to the extent that we have faith in them and believe that they work. They are vehicles of intent, not the important thing, although they can be useful, just as a car can be useful to take us to our destination once we decide where we want to go. But the important thing is the decision, the irrevocable decision, to change our luck – not the vehicle we use to implement it.

Changing our luck basically involves two things: visualization and appreciation.

Much has been written about visualization (see e.g. Shakti Gawain's *Creative Visualization* or my book *Thought Forms*), so only a few points will be mentioned here.

Visualization is similar to normal daydreaming, except the latter is done with thinking, and the former is done with feeling. Daydreaming is done in the third person and the future tense, whereas visualization is done in the first person and the present tense. In visualization you imagine yourself to be actually in the middle of the scene as if it were unfolding around you here and now; and you let yourself feel all the joy you would feel if that scene were actually happening. The secret of visualization is to convince yourself that what you are wishing for is already true – to vividly imagine yourself in the middle of the scenario of your desire coming true – and to allow yourself to feel the feelings you would feel if that were in fact the case.

Also, visualization should not be overly specific. For example, "winning the lottery" is a silly thing to wish for or to visualize. It's too specific, too confining to the Spirit – as if one were trying to dictate to it. "Wealth" or better yet, "Freedom from money worries" is a better thing to visualize because it gives the Spirit more free play, more liberty to send us suggestions on how to achieve wealth. Similarly, to wish that Mary or John would fall in love with us is too specific, and verges on black magic. It's better to just visualize love from some unnamed person, since if all we want specifically is John's love or Mary's love, then we'll reject Sam's love or Judy's love when it is offered to us – perfectly good love, but not our specific image of what we thought we wanted.

Luck means letting the Spirit bring us what we want in its own way, in its own time. This doesn't mean we sit on our hands and vegetate; it just means keeping open to different possibilities as they arise, rather than clinging to some specific payoff (image of what we think it is we want).

The other thing we need to change our luck is appreciation, which means appreciating what we already have – considering ourselves to be already lucky, rather than already unlucky. This isn't too hard to do: we live in a beautiful world, in a wealthy country, in a time of relative peace and prosperity; we have enough to eat, we are educated and have millions of opportunities at hand. If we don't already consider ourselves to be damned lucky, then we ought to be ashamed of ourselves.

One good technique for learning appreciation is by gratefully comparing ourselves to people who are worse off than we are (just turn on the news!); rather than jealously comparing ourselves to people who are better off than we are. What we are aiming for in both visualization and in appreciating what we already have is a joyous, optimistic, expectant attitude. Although it takes a good attitude to have a good attitude, it doesn't necessarily take a good attitude to *want* a good attitude. When our desire to have a good attitude, no matter what is happening to us, exceeds our desire for some certain thing to happen, THEN our luck will start to change.

If we just keep plugging away, at a certain point we come to realize that what we really want isn't health or wealth or love from other people, but rather happiness, contentment in our own hearts. We come to understand that the health or wealth or love is only a symbol for what we really want, which is to be joyous unto ourselves for no particular reason at all. The health or wealth or love we visualized so intensely for so long doesn't have anything to do with it except as sort of a mnemonic device, like the beads on a rosary. We find we can be joyous in our visualizations and in our appreciation of what we already have – we don't even need the visualizations to come true in order to be happy. It's at this point that our luck will start to change, and the visualizations will come true.

Spirit Possession

The subject of spirit possession is not well understood in our society; moreover, it has a somewhat unsavory connotation and is not mentioned openly, nor considered a serious topic for discussion. In fact, lots of people are possessed by spirits without knowing it. In this essay we will take a quick survey of the whole subject of possession. The subject of spirit possession has implications for a proper understanding of both cognition – the nature of consciousness – and of comparative religion.

From the point of view of comparative religion, the common denominator in most religions is channeling information and guidance from spirits. The form of this channeling may vary from place to place; and of course the spirits being invoked vary from religion to religion; but the basic technique of spirit communication and interaction is pretty much the same throughout the world.

For example, the Catholic mass is an invocation of Jesus and the Holy Spirit; and the Jewish Passover Seder includes an invocation of Elijah. It is because the form of spirit communication is mandated by the spirits involved themselves that religious ceremonies the world over tend to be very similar in their rituals: darkened rooms, candles and incense, repetitive litanies, etc. These techniques, which derive from shamanism, put participants in a light trance state to make them more receptive to the spirits' messages. Trance channeling can be considered a temporary manifestation of spirit possession. Priesthood is an example of benign spirit possession: priests are able to perform magical operations (such as healing and casting out demons) because they can call upon the power of the spirits of their religion (Jesus, Buddha, Krishna, whomever) who possess them to assist them in these tasks.

From the point of view of consciousness, spirit possession is a fact which must be reckoned with in our calculations. Merely because the society we live in pretends that spirit possession doesn't exist doesn't mean that spirit possession doesn't exist. As the essay Channeling Spirit Guides says, all we really are is a flux of thought forms (images, opinions, beliefs, and expectations learned from our parents and society) which is being urged this way and that by spirit forces.

The most common form of possession – which is also the most dangerous – is not spirit possession, but rather possession by other people. This is because in the entire universe, including all the hell worlds, there are no demons which are as malignant, tenacious, and gratuitously cruel as are our fellow humans.

Possession by other people occurs whenever we let them impose their feelings upon us. Any time we allow ourselves to feel another person's mood, we are temporarily possessed by that person. When we experience a great work of art, or even a gripping TV show, we are allowing ourselves to be possessed by the artist, and by the spirits who inspired him or her.

Most children are possessed by their parents unless they're super-rebellious hellions from the cradle on, and most marriages are a species of mutual possession. This type of possession is called "being under the shadow" of another person. This is not necessarily a bad thing; all forms of apprenticeship and learning involve putting oneself under another person's shadow. What is being passed from the teacher to the learner is wholly subconscious and emotional; i.e., possession entails a direct transference of knowledge (assurance), no matter what intellectual symbols – beliefs or techniques – it may be wrapped up in. To be possessed by another person means to allow oneself to be emotionally directed by that person.

Being under the shadow of another person only becomes detrimental when the shadow is imposed by coercion, through fear or guilt. Most parent / child relationships and marriages have at least a tinge of these elements. Basically the only way of casting off the shadow of another person (once it's in place) is by diminishing our own self-importance, so the other person is left with nothing to manipulate. It is usually much more difficult, traumatic, time-consuming, and painful to cast off the shadow of another person than it is to exorcise a demon.

Demon possession is also a common form of possession. Most of the people who are habitually, obsessively angry, fearful, repressed, depressed, irritable, self-destructive, chronically ill, etc. are demon-possessed. Mainstream psychotherapy's rejection of the notion of demon possession is totally absurd: it's like trying to formulate a science of physics while rejecting the calculus – you can still do it, but are handicapping yourself unnecessarily. Practically all neuroses and personality disorders are symptoms of demon possession, and while they can be treated without reference to the underlying problem, this is not a very skillful way of doing it.

People call demons in to possess them when they feel vulnerable and in need of drastic protection and security. Demons give them strength – rationalizations, shamelessness, hard-heartedness, self-pity – with which to fend off the attacks of other people and the buffeting of circumstances. An infant may call a demon in at birth to protect him from his parents; a dying person may call one in to dull the emotions in the face of overwhelming fear. Demons can be called in any time to cover vulnerability with hardness. Usually the decision to call in a demon is made in dreamless sleep (i.e. unconsciously).

Here is a fictional example of demon possession from the children's book *Harriet the Spy* by Louise Fitzhugh, which shows how people call demons in to possess them at moments of great vulnerability and self-pity. In the story Harriet has just been rejected – deservedly – by all of her friends:

"She sat very stupidly with a blank mind until finally 'I feel different' came slowly into her head. ... 'Yes', she thought, after a long pause. And then, after more time, 'Mean, I feel mean.'

"She looked around with a mean look for everyone. Nobody saw her. She felt her face contorting. It was an impressive moment that everyone missed. It was a moment that Harriet would never forget.

"When the bell rang for lunch, it was as though she didn't have to think any more. Everything happened as though she had planned it but she really hadn't. For example, when the bell rang Pinky Whitehead jumped up and ran down the aisle. Harriet put her foot out and he fell flat on his face.

"A terrific wail went up from his prone body, and when he raised his face his nose was bleeding. Harriet looked extremely blank. Inside she felt a sense of very personal satisfaction."

Note that calling a demon in unconsciously, in a thoughtless fit of undisciplined anger or self-pity, has all the consequences of conscious demon-possession (the demon won't leave unless deliberately exorcised).

In fact, our society is founded upon demonism. The fundamentalist Christians are quite correct in their appraisal of the extent to which Satan and his minions run our society. All our closed-heartedness to one another – the hard-edged snarl that underlies most of our interactions with other people – is urged on us by demon "advisors". The cartoon stereotype of a little angel and devil perched on the shoulders of a character alternately whispering in his ears, is 100% accurate. Psychopaths are extreme examples of demon possession (not much humanity left there at all), but actually we're all like that just beneath the surface, which is why we're so fascinated by gruesome news stories: that's us. We're all allowing ourselves to be swayed by the blandishments of demons all the time, even if we're not actually possessed by them, and the psychos we see on the news are just acting it out openly for everyone else. For example, when we are driving and another driver cuts in right ahead of us and we beep the horn in anger, that's in fact an exchange between that guy's demons and our own. Our anger is like a little snack to the demons who hover around us constantly like mosquitoes waiting for a little dart of anger, fear, etc. they can suck.

Only people who are completely at peace in their own hearts are not supplying fodder to the demons who coinhabit our sphere and live off of the seething emotions generated by the frustration and despair which living in an unjust society (such as ours) produces. In a just society people are happy, and therefore produce little demon-food; and as a result such societies are not run by or bothered by demons. This whole "problem of evil" jazz can be easily sidestepped just by not harboring evil intentions in our hearts, and by treating other people in the same way that we'd prefer they treated us.

Now, possession can be defined as the delegation of responsibility for making decisions. Nowadays our tendency is to allow ourselves to be possessed by society – i.e. to let society decide everything for us. This is so extraordinarily commonplace that we take it for granted, but in fact the overwhelming majority of what we call "our" feelings (like about 99.999%) are just the feelings of other people – parents, spouse, boss, teachers, peers, the media – which we have accepted as our own. Practically everything we like, dislike, desire, fear, sympathize with, disdain, etc. is just what we've learned to like, dislike, desire, fear, sympathize with, or disdain. Advertising and politics are the two sciences of societal possession. Society has us repress our own true feelings and dictates what we "should" feel instead. About the only feeling it lets us feel for ourselves is pain. Societal possession is the default option for people not possessed by spirits.

Actually it is not society which possesses us, since society has no soul, but rather our own thought forms (habits and predilections) which are shaped by society. Everything we have learned since the moment we were born is a thought form; and these thought forms are beings with volitions all their own. This is why our habits and thoughts seem so uncontrollable to us – thought forms do indeed have wills of their own which can be at variance with ours. Thought forms are not evil – without them we'd be as helpless as newborns – and it's quite possible to utilize thought forms skillfully. We don't have to be mindless robots operating on social (thought form) programming. In other words, we don't have to delegate unconditional decision-making power to our thought forms.

As is the case with all forms of possession, thought form (societal) possession is in essence a trade: we trade power to our thought forms, namely the power to make decisions for us; and they give us power in return, in this case, the power to act in society. Basically, the power we receive from any form of possession is the suspension of doubt. E.g. our belief that society works (can be depended on to deliver the goods for us) is the result of our possession by our own thought forms.

Of course the only reason it works is because of our collective belief that it works. Society – our possession by our thought forms – depends upon our credulity, our willingness to put all doubts aside and give our hearts and minds to a system of belief without examining it too closely. The reason we have difficulty making spirituality (trust in the Spirit instead of society) work at first is because of our initial doubt that it works, which is the residual effect of our possession by society.

The reason we get on the spiritual path in the first place – no matter whether magical or Christian or Buddhist or whatever – is because of our realization that society doesn't work. Doubt creeps in and undermines our possession by society's thought forms. We realize that although society has a lot of neat tricks up its sleeve, happiness is nowhere among them. At that point we have to conjure up new thought forms – ideals and beliefs – to possess us; otherwise we'd go stark, raving nuts, as some people do when they realize that society has "failed" them.

The point is that possession by society, like all forms of possession, gives us a sense of direction and purpose in life – an orientation and a force of will (lack of doubt) to sustain us. And, like all other forms of possession, it can easily enslave us.

Some societal possession does have a spiritual basis. Obsession with money is often the result and cause of possession by Mammon; and many drunks are possessed by Bacchus. This is no metaphor; these sorts of deities indeed exist, in the same sense and to the same degree that Bill Gates, for example, exists; and they do indeed possess their votaries. Neither Mammon nor Bacchus are intrinsically evil spirits;

rather, a stout heart is required to resist enslavement by the power of any spirit, even a good one.

In contrast to demon possession and societal (thought form) possession, which are usually unconscious, unskillful manifestations of possession, the spiritual path is the conscious acknowledgment and employment of possession as a tool. For people on the spiritual path who don't have human gurus, spirit possession is about the only avenue open to self-transformation. The spiritual path is sufficiently complex an undertaking – a maze with so many dead-ends, and requiring so much strength of will – that few people could succeed in following it without the guidance and power obtained from a possessing agent, either a human guru, or a spirit.

Most religions recognize this, and provide a ritual for calling in a possessing spirit. In Christianity, the aspirant is called to "make the decision for Jesus" or "invite Jesus into one's life" or "ask Jesus to come live inside one". When the aspirant makes such a firm decision of his or her own free will, he or she is at that moment possessed by Jesus (or rather by the Holy Spirit, which is directed by Jesus). Similarly, the Buddhist aspirant is exhorted to "take refuge in the Buddha, Dharma, and Sangha". The act of "taking refuge" is the same thing as inviting the Buddha to take possession.

Two points to remember about spirit possession are 1) spirits, whether good or evil, can only possess a host by invitation; although many people who are possessed by demons invited the demons in dreamless sleep – i.e. the invitation doesn't have to be conscious; and 2) spirits can be exorcised by the same process of firm decision to cast them out as was used to invite them in.

Like everything else, spirit possession has its advantages and disadvantages. For a person on the spiritual path who does not have a human guru, possession by a beneficent spirit such as Jesus, Buddha, Krishna, etc. is de rigueur. The spiritual path is just too tortuous and tricky to manage without a navigator who is outside of and above us, and who can take a detached and long-term view. Indeed, the essential thing on the spiritual path is relinquishment of ones' own will (decision-making). Ironically, although possession can facilitate the relinquishment of self-will, when abused it has the effect of increasing self-will.

To be possessed by a spirit is to tap into a source of great power, and few people have the sobriety and calm to withstand enslavement by this power. Jesus, for example, is most certainly a good spirit; yet it is also true that some people who are possessed by him become intoxicated with power – with the certainty of their own salvation, with the imminent triumph of their dogma, with the compulsion to shove their trip down other people's throats. This isn't Jesus' fault: he certainly tries to steer his votaries in the right direction. Nor can he unilaterally withdraw his power from those who abuse it: possession is a contract which can only by terminated from the human side. Neither Jesus, nor Mammon or Bacchus for that matter, call on their votaries to destroy other people; but this has been the not infrequent result of possession by them (only demons call for the out-and-out destruction of others).

Being possessed by a beneficent spirit is like having a bracing tonic for the heart and nerves available at hand whenever needed, to get through the spiritually dry periods when we feel like throwing up our arms in exasperation and crying, "How long, O Lord, how long?" At those times it's helpful to be possessed by a spirit, because there's comfort in the sense that although everything may be spinning out of control, there's somebody up there somewhere who understands what's happening and whispers in our ears, "Leave the driving to us."

I, personally, am possessed by a group of deities who belong to the pantheon of the indigenous people where I live (Central America). I was originally working with these deities in a more casual fashion, with regard to agriculture, when my spirit guides suggested that I invite them to possess me, and I did so (spirit guides are just that – guides. They have neither the power nor inclination to possess humans). These deities help me in various ways. They prop me up – help me accomplish things that I could not normally do by myself. For example, they taught me how to hold my attention fixed on a single feeling moment-to-moment, all day long, every day. At first they lent me their power, so in the beginning I found the exercise remarkably easy; then little-by-little they withdrew their power, which made the thing progressively harder and harder to do, but still doable, until I was able to do it by myself.

Another thing they've done on occasion is show me scenes from my past and future in my mind's eye, but incredibly vivid and emotionally compelling, not unlike what the ghosts of Christmas past, present, and future did to Ebenezer Scrooge.

Also, the frequency and intensity of omens and portents in my life seem to have jumped exponentially ever since these deities took over the controls. And they talk to me and tell me about all sorts of things, like agriculture, divination, healing, etc. They also have introduced me to some interesting people. And they come to me in dreams and show me things. Actually, they're a trip. But beyond the weird stuff, they're also good friends. I trust them and feel comfortable in their presence; and they're omnipresent.

The relationship between humans and spirits is symbiotic. Possessing humans gives spirits embodied agents in the physical world through whom the spirits can extend the range of their activities. Spirits cannot act directly upon the physical world (actually, they can here and there, e.g. poltergeists, but it's pretty spasmodic). All spirits can do by themselves is wait until a fortuitous juxtaposition of circumstances pops up, and then give things a little tangential shove this way or that. But they are not capable of acting in the world in a sustained, methodical fashion; for that they need human (or animal, or vegetable, or mineral) agents.

The dilemma for the aspirant is that the spiritual path requires calmness, gentleness, and humility; and spirit possession militates against the development of these qualities. On the other hand, the spiritual path also requires fierce determination and an unwavering sense of direction, which are really only available by means of some form of possession. A human guru tries to prevent his or her disciples from indulging in excesses by constantly kicking the legs out from under their self-importance (which is why e.g. don Juan, Sri Yukteswar, Gurdjieff, etc. were so harsh and abusive to their disciples); but with spirit possession there are no such restraints. On the other hand, in this day and age there are very few true gurus out there, so the aspirant on the spiritual path has to make use of what tools are available.

Being possessed by a spirit is like packing a loaded pistol. Some people get a real charge out of having a gun in their hands, and it makes them act in all kinds of crazy and stupid ways. People like that are a real danger to themselves and to others. But there is such a thing as responsible gun handling; and there is such a thing as responsible spirit possession.

The widespread fear and condemnation of spirit possession in our society is complete hypocrisy, considering the sizable percentage of the population which is possessed. Just as up until very recently society made us feel ashamed of our sexuality, so too does society make us fear a perfectly ordinary and commonplace phenomenon such as spirit possession. It's about time everyone came out of the closet and copped to what's really going on.

Two Kinds of Hurt

There are two kinds of hurt: self-pitying hurt and sad hurt. Self-pitying hurt is the kind of hurt we feel on purpose, so that we'll have a good excuse to wallow in self-pity. Whenever we are self-righteously indignant at someone else's behavior, we are indulging in self-pitying hurt. We seek self-pitying hurt when we expect or demand something from another person which that person is not offering freely. Whenever we believe that other people (e.g. our parents, spouse, or children) owe us anything; whenever we try to bribe, wheedle, or coerce other people; to try to make them feel guilty if they don't come across for us; to impose our own desires on them beyond what they are comfortable with; then what we are actually seeking from them is their rejection, which we can conveniently blame on them.

Whenever we make our happiness depend on something which someone else does or doesn't do, we are just asking that person to hurt us. This kind of hurt is easily avoided by being respectful of other people's space: their limits, their right to have feelings of their own, *including the right to reject us*, if they so desire, without our resenting, denying it, or taking it as a personal affront.

Where self-pitying hurt is the natural consequence of possessive love, sad hurt is the doorway to true love. Sad hurt is the hurt which other people make us feel in spite of our having reached out to them joyously and in good faith. Sad hurt is puzzling hurt (as opposed to self-righteous hurt). Where self-pitying hurt can easily be avoided by listening to and respecting other people's feelings, sad hurt is unavoidable – it's part and parcel of the human condition. Sad hurt is the hurt which other people lay on us purposely – the product of their self-hatred which they project onto us as scapegoats. Sad hurt is the hurt we feel when other people are just using us as an excuse to pity themselves.

This kind of hurt seems very unjust and unfair; and it *is* unjust and unfair. Although it is a meager consolation, this kind of "unmerited" hurt is indeed the result of karma that we ourselves set into motion in other lifetimes and realities. If we feel that it is unjust that we should have to suffer now for sins committed in other lifetimes, that's too bad; but it's life, and there's no use complaining about it. Complaining is what turns it into self-pitying hurt.

When other people try purposely to hurt us, it hurts. There's no use pretending that it doesn't hurt, or getting angry at them in return. Those responses (apathy or anger) cover our feelings of sad hurt – keep us from feeling the hurt directly by substituting thought forms of self-pity for the direct perception of pain. These are our protections (closing up or striking back) when other people deliberately try to hurt us, and they are effective blocks against the feeling of sad hurt. However, they also block out the feeling of true love.

If we're going to be open to other people's love, we have to be open to their hurt as well. Vulnerability is not a door that can be opened and closed selectively, to let some feelings through and not others. To protect ourselves from feeling hurt is to prevent ourselves from feeling love.

When the crowd taunted and crucified Jesus, he felt deeply, deeply hurt. He felt exactly the same way we would feel if there was a crowd of people taunting us and pouring their self-hatred upon us, and we had done nothing to deserve it. Jesus was not such an exalted being that he no longer had a capacity to feel hurt. On the contrary, he was an exalted being precisely because he let himself feel the hurt directly, instead of blocking his pain with self-pity (apathy or anger).

No matter how enlightened we may become, we never get to a place where hurt no longer hurts. There's no way that hurt ever does anything except feel BAD. But if someone hurts us and we let ourselves feel the hurt directly, then that's that; that's the way the cookie crumbles. We feel bad for a little while, and then the feeling passes and we go on to something else.

But if we are afraid to feel hurt directly; if we reject the feeling of hurt by substituting apathy or anger for it, by trying to dominate or control relationships, by rolling over and playing the victim right off the top, or by avoiding intimacy altogether; then we are in fact grabbing onto our hurt, hugging it to our bosoms, and making it the centerpiece of all our relationships. And all there can ever be is hurt, because we leave no room for love to get in anywhere – we've got every chink stuffed.

Apathy and anger aren't really painkillers, they're just pain deferrers. All they do is postpone the pain. The only way to really get through pain, to get over it and past it, is by feeling it directly. Of course, this is the last thing which people who are in pain want to hear: "Haven't I suffered enough?" they ask. "And it's not even my fault!" But the truth is that the amount of pain which people feel (or repress into apathy or anger) is the precise amount of pain which they must yet feel to disentangle themselves from it and put the pain behind them.

This is because pain is not something which is external (imposed from without), but rather arises from within ourselves. The external situation which causes pain is but a symbol for something going on inside us on an emotional level. To consider our pain as something detached from ourselves is to refuse responsibility for our pain. To blame someone else for our pain, to try to make someone else take responsibility for feeling our pain, is futile. Only by feeling our pain directly, looking within ourselves for the source of our pain, are we taking responsibility for it, and thereby putting ourselves in a position to move beyond it. We do this by finding a way to heal our own wounds, instead of expecting or demanding other people to heal them for us. Other people *can't* heal us; they're in too much pain themselves to have any extra love to spare. We have to be willing to take complete responsibility for our own healing.

Go back in your mind's eye to every scene in your life when you were hurt by other people. You do this like a normal daydream or fantasy, but instead of trying to capture a feeling of glory, vindication, self-righteousness, etc. (as is done in normal daydreaming), you try to capture the feeling of hurt that you felt at that time. Watch the scene of that person who is you being rejected and needing love, and give love to that person. Talk to the you in the visualization, call to him or her: "There, there, cheer up! You may have been rejected, but you're still a worthwhile person. You'll go on living and breathing, and in time you'll find true love. After all, I love you. I really do!"

Say this using your own words and sentiments, and mean what you say. Give yourself all the sympathy and compassion that you were denied at that time. Let yourself feel sad for that person who is you. And when you let yourself feel sad for yourself, you'll also find yourself feeling sad for the people who hurt you.

Sad hurt implies forgiveness – the sadness is as much for those who hurt us as it is for ourselves. Sadness, not anger, is the true feeling we share with the people who hurt us. Anger separates us from them, whereas sadness unites us to them – we are one with them in sadness.

This visualization is not so different from what we do when we indulge ourselves in angry fantasies of the people who have hurt us – telling them off, or delighting when they feel remorse for what they've done to us. But instead of using the visualization to stoke our self-pity, we use it to heal ourselves by feeling good about who we are.

To be able to love others and to freely receive their love in return, we have to be ready to be rejected and hurt by them. We have to be willing to face this directly, instead of preparing ourselves in advance, bracing ourselves, taking out insurance in advance against hurt. We have to be able to forgive people for the bad things they do to us rather than get into a tizzy about it – forgive them because they don't know what they're doing.

Of course, this is a lot easier said than done, but the key to it is being willing to feel hurt: not angry and vindictive, not blithely pretending we're not hurt, not bitterly wallowing in self-pity over past hurt, not setting up ground rules and strictures in relationships to guard against the possibility of future hurt; but just plain old feel hurt. If we can truly open ourselves up to hurt, then we'll automatically open ourselves up to love.

Acting With The Spirit

There are two ways of getting what we want from life: raping it, or seducing it; that is to say, acting on our thought forms (our socially conditioned beliefs and expectations), or acting with the Spirit. The former mode is the way of the average person, and the latter is the way of the magician. Because these two modes of action are entwined, the neophyte magician often finds it difficult to determine when an impulse to action truly comes from the Spirit, and when it's just thought forms (ego games).

The chief feature which distinguishes acting with the Spirit from acting on thought forms is patience, and this patience is a product of humility. This patience means understanding that we are not a special case, that the universe is not going to bend itself around us, that the Spirit doesn't care whether we are the CEO of XYZ Corp., or saved by Jesus, or a 93rd degree magus in the Mystical Order of the Platinum Pumpernickel. No matter how hot stuff we think we are, to the Spirit we're just one of the gang.

Note that this is exactly the opposite of the way we are trained to act in society. Our thought form training leads us to feel that we're so damned important. Society trains us to believe that we deserve this and this and this – that stifling all our true feelings at society's behest and turning ourselves into mindless robots to serve society's ends gives us some kind of rights in the matter. But this is an illusion. To the Spirit, our little lives and our little pain are of zero importance whatsoever. As long as we feel that the Spirit owes us something, that we deserve special treatment or consideration because of how noble and spiritual we are, or how much we've suffered, then we are acting on thought forms and not with the Spirit. Acting with the Spirit means going to the end of the line and patiently waiting our turn.

See, if we're dissatisfied with how the Spirit is handling our accounts, then right off the top we're not acting with the Spirit. The first principle of acting with the Spirit is to be satisfied with how the Spirit is dealing with us *right now*. This means taking responsibility for our karma, for the situation in which we find ourselves; trying to understand what lessons we're seeking to learn through our experience, instead of trying to escape from it into some rosy daydreamed future. Acting with the Spirit means understanding that life is something we do, not something that just happens to us.

The question arises, if we cannot wheedle or cajole the Spirit, how can we seduce it? Or another way of asking this is: if we cannot use the future as an escape hatch, how can we nonetheless manipulate it to our advantage? The answer is that there is actually no such thing as "the future" in the sense in which we are accustomed to thinking of it – i.e. as a linear series of events which takes off from this moment. Rather, there are an infinite number of futures (called probable realities) which take off right from this moment. "The future" is not so much a straight path as it is an infinitely ramified hall of mirrors.

BANG! You're dead! That was one probable reality right there. Luckily you missed that one; but someone didn't. Somebody else who wasn't expecting it either got theirs right there and then.

The point is that what we are attempting to do with magic is to pick that one of the infinite probable realities which branch off from the present moment which will lead to a future in which we realize our desires. The problem is that our thinking minds, which can only process thought forms (not feelings), are not smart enough to make the right connections, to be able to pick out the right decision in the now moment that will lead us to the probable reality in which our desires come true. We can't see that picking up that piece of trash off the street and depositing it in a waste can was the decision which led (maybe years down the line) to our receiving that promotion or winning the lottery or finding true love.

Moreover, the Spirit is a trickster, always testing our resolve. It always disguises the decision in the now moment which will bring us what we desire in the future as something which strikes us as disagreeable. The Spirit sets things up so that we will tend to reject the very probable reality which would bring us what we truly want. It dangles what we want right before our eyes and then jerks it away at the last minute; or makes us keep on keeping on way past what we thought we were capable of. A true gift of the Spirit always requires us to go an extra mile; to follow a gleam of hope in the midst of defeat; to confront the impossible with complete élan.

In order to win the Spirit over, then, we must show it that we mean business. In order to consciously choose which probable reality we find ourselves in (instead of just letting the random throw of the dice determine it), *we must stick to our decisions*. If we make a firm, irrevocable decision (whether consciously or unconsciously) and we stick to it through thick and thin, then we will eventually wind up in the probable reality in which that decision comes true.

Note that average people don't usually do this. They are basically only interested in keeping comfortable, and whining and complaining when they're not. They don't have the will necessary to stand by their decisions. To accomplish anything in life – even just running in place – requires unwavering determination.

It is helpful to the neophyte magician to read autobiographies of people who succeeded in getting the Spirit to cough up what they wanted. Such books as *The Spirit of St. Louis* by Charles Lindbergh, *Act One* by Moss Hart, *Be My Guest* by Conrad Hilton, and *My Early Life* by Winston Churchill (especially the "Escape from the Boers" chapters), are excellent treatises on magic written by competent practitioners of the art of acting with the Spirit. These guys were dreamers, but they weren't *idle* dreamers. They didn't sit around wishin' and hopin' and thinkin' and prayin' for the Spirit to pass a miracle for them. Facing certain defeat they didn't wring their hands helplessly or throw in the towel. Rather, they stood up defiantly and grasped their destiny by the horns, took complete responsibility for making their dreams come true, and passed miracles by themselves. They became one with the Spirit.

Magic isn't a matter of wearing funny clothes and reciting funny chants – waving a wand and reciting a formula and making the Spirit jump at your command. Rather, it's a matter of patience and determination. How can you expect to bend the universe to your will when you can't even control your own thoughts and emotions, your own doubts and fears and inertia?

When you know in your heart that *you* are the author of your present situation; that nothing is going to change in your life until *you* make the decision to change; that *you* must take complete responsibility for your own destiny; then you are acting with the Spirit. When you feel the inner peace which only comes from the knowledge that you have done everything humanly possible and let the chips fall where they may; then you are one with the Spirit.

Spiritual Cookery

I then asked [Dr. Steiner], *"How can it happen that the spiritual impulse, and especially the inner schooling, for which you are constantly providing stimulus and guidance bear so little fruit? Why do the people concerned give so little evidence of spiritual experience, in spite of all their efforts? Why, worst of all, is the will for action, for the carrying out of these spiritual impulses, so weak?"*

Then came the thought-provoking and surprising answer: "This is a problem of nutrition. Nutrition as it is today does not supply the strength necessary for manifesting the spirit in physical life. A bridge can no longer be built from thinking to will and action."

— Ehrenfried Pfeiffer, from the introduction to *Agriculture – Eight Lectures by Rudolf Steiner*

We all know that "you are what you eat"; and many of us are becoming aware that this maxim has a spiritual as well as a physical dimension. We know we simply feel better when we eat well – when our bodies, rather than our minds, dictate what we should eat or not eat. Many of us have experienced a complete change in attitude and outlook on life by simply changing our diets. Whole bodies of thought, such as the Jewish kosher laws and macrobiotics, have evolved to stress the spirituality of food, to emphasize its sacredness.

The "spiritual quality of food" is not a metaphor: food contains a light fiber energy which is as important to our sustenance as vitamins and proteins, but which is not susceptible to chemical analysis. And just as the vitamin and protein content of food can be diminished by processing or overcooking, so too can the light fiber content of food be diminished by *disrespect*.

Light fibers are actually the same things as good feelings. When we feel good, we literally glow. When a food plant or animal feels good, it glows. Even when it is killed for food, the glow remains as long as the killing was done with respect; that is, with a sense of connectedness and gratitude rather than mechanically.

A farmer puts the glow into his plants and animals by treating them with respect – by respecting their feelings. Practically all farmers farm for the love of it; they sure don't do it for the money. They feel joyous as they ride their tractors up and down their fields, and that good feeling is communicated to the soil and plants. Similarly, most dairy farmers not only address their cows as individuals, but they also develop quirky personal relationships with them. Therefore, from a light fiber point of view, our vegetable and milk supplies are still relatively safe. Most egg farms, on the other hand, are run like Auschwitz, and that's what makes eggs poisonous to eat (not their cholesterol).

Not all cultures have been so cut off from their true feelings about food as ours is today. Many Native American tribes had a deep awareness that they were a part of what they ate – e.g., the buffalo. They lived with the buffalo, followed the buffalo, prayed to the buffalo. They were one with the buffalo, and thus to them eating was a sacrament. Modern Native Americans maintain that same attitude of reverence towards maize.

But in America today we mine food, extract the nutrients out of it, strip it, rape it, and throw it away. What little nourishment for the spirit is left in food by modern agricultural and processing methods is completely destroyed by the way we eat it. We use food in a most disrespectful manner – stuffing it in gluttonously whether we are hungry or not, whether it tastes good or not, whether we really want it or not; and then we waste food as if to piss on it. Like sex, we have turned eating from a joyous, spiritual act into a source of great shame.

An infant doesn't conceive of his food or his mother as something separate from himself; he doesn't feel more important than his food, and therefore doesn't feel disconnected from it. When an infant eats, he mingles with his food: he touches it, gets to know how it feels. It's pretty, it satisfies his hunger, it makes him happy. But when an infant first sees adults eat, it makes him feel shame. This is because we adults don't identify with our food – it's as if our food is not a part of us, as if what we are putting into our mouths is something foreign to ourselves. We attack our food as if it is separate from us, and it is the act of eating which allows us to use it. We bite it off in huge mouthfuls like ravenous hyenas, chew it and swallow it with gulps of contempt. We come together in great rituals like Thanksgiving and Christmas in which we engage in orgies of gluttony and wastefulness to jointly validate our shame, all the while calling it glory. And that lie makes us even more ashamed; so we lie about that one too, and call it glory. And so on. And nobody will look at what they are really feeling, because if being pigs has brought us glory, why look at what pigs we are?

The reason why saints can survive on so little food is because they're not attacking it, squeezing the life out of it, so it takes very little to sustain them. The Native Americans are able to survive on a diet of pretty much nothing but corn because they love the corn, and the corn loves them back, and they're able to live from that love even though from the point of view of nutrition they should slowly starve to death.

While it is true that the original light fiber energy in food can be vitiated by disrespect anywhere along the line – in handling, processing, cooking, or eating – it is also true that light fiber energy, being more flexible than vitamins or proteins, can be restored to food by respecting and treating it as sacred – by ritualizing the activities connected with it.

First of all, it's important that you should raise at least some of your own food, even if all this means is a couple of pots of herbs or jars of sprouts grown on a window shelf. Try to throw in at least a pinch of home-grown herbs or sprouts into every meal you cook (not necessarily every dish, but every meal). Visualize yourself casting fibers of light into the food as you add your home-grown herbs or produce.

Next, bless your key, staple ingredients – salt, flour, sugar, honey, etc. You can ask any spirit helpers you are presently using to do this for you: Jesus or Mary, Krishna, nature spirits, etc. can all do the job for you. Just take them a pound of sugar, salt, or flour; address them in whatever form you are accustomed to; and ask them to please bless your ingredients. If you don't have a spirit helper, just take the ingredients to the summit of the largest or most imposing mountain or hill in your immediate area; take the mountain spirit a token portion of something special you have cooked yourself as an offering; and ask him or her to please bless your ingredients. Don't worry about whether you are doing it right: if you are doing it in good faith, you're doing it right.

Keep your sacred, blessed ingredients apart from the regular ones, but whenever you refill the sugar bowl, salt shaker, flour bin, etc. add a pinch of the blessed ingredient, and imagine that you are putting light fibers in with the pinch.

Observe that you must never be in a bad mood when you cook, nor must you eat food cooked by someone who is in a bad mood, or even an indifferent one. A burger from a McDonald's where the employees are a light, happy bunch has more light fiber energy than a plate of organic brown rice from a vegetarian restaurant where the cook is bored or is angry at the manager.

You can easily tell when food has bad vibes. It's not that it tastes bad per se; rather, it feels wrong or out of place in your mouth – there's no incentive to chew it and swallow it. Whenever you get a feeling like this about something you are eating, spit it out. Don't swallow it, even to be polite. Much processed, convenience food "tastes" like this – bland, insipid, effete, enervated – but people get so used to this kind of food that they can't tell the difference any more. They just assume that feeling lousy all the time is how you're supposed to feel, and they cease to notice that it is their food which is bringing them down.

Finally, talk to your food. Thank it as if it were alive and could understand you. Not long conversation, just a simple acknowledgment that you are aware of being in the presence of a sentient being who is worthy of your respect, who died for you, and from whom you wish a favor. You wouldn't ask a human being for a favor in a surly, disrespectful manner; on the contrary, you would ask humbly and respectfully, and feel gratitude for the favor when granted. And that is how you must address your food: take small bites, chew it slowly and mindfully, eat in silence paying attention to the act of eating, and never eat until full.

Eating Recommendations

With the possible exception of sex, eating is the most powerful act you perform in your daily life. Yet in our society (assuming that you are not e.g. a kosher Jew or a macrobiotic) most of us tend to trivialize this act – indeed, to feel ashamed of it (just as society has taught us to be ashamed of sex). Every bite you take either clogs your body or gives it lightness. Take no bite for its sweetness or pleasant flavor. Every bit you take in must be weighed, and every word you speak must be measured.

Foods (except for salads) should not be mixed together. Foods should be treated with respect, as if they had an integrity of their own. It's not wise to use a lot of condiments such as soy sauce, catsup, Worcestershire, or wine; although they can be used sparingly. Butter on top of things is okay. Foods shouldn't be boiled and boiled (such as tomato sauce) – evaporated is better. Herbs are fine, but not lots of them mixed up. One or at most two herbs per dish. Sesame can be sprinkled over things, but not enough so you can really feel it. Just a hint – that's the secret – just a hint. Garlic has good healing properties, but just a hint. Not lots of salt on things. Bread is okay (except for people with a lot of mucus), but it should be kept simple: water, yeast, salt, flour – period, not a lot of additives. Fresh-squeezed juices are excellent. Sugar is like salt – okay in small quantities. Same with soy sauce and black and chile pepper. All of these things are okay in small quantities to add an accent and heighten the taste of foods, not to swamp them.

Mayonnaise should be made fresh each time, with lemon juice (not vinegar). In fact, lemon juice should be used in preference to vinegar in all cases, except when lemons are unobtainable. Honey is better than sugar in all cases where substitution is possible; but price, convenience, or flavor may determine sugar use instead. It's best to use little salt; try using herbs instead. Herbs should be an accent, not a strong flavor. Use more of them in preference to soy sauce, bouillon, etc. Use melted butter over things in preference to heavy white sauces. Food should be light: heavy, doughy things like pasta casseroles, doughnuts, warm bread, starch puddings, peanut butter, even potatoes, make people sluggish and dull. Even bread should be a once or twice a week thing, not a feature at every meal. Chicken and fish should be used in preference to red meats, and even those very sparingly.

People who have high blood pressure (or diabetes) who are forbidden to eat salt (or sugar) and who miss these things in their diets can do a little trick which is based on the same principle as homeopathic medicine: take one part salt (or sugar) and ten parts flour and mix them together well. Repeat this procedure five or six times, until you have a mixture that is less than one part per million salt. Then, just use this as you would use normal table salt: put it in a shaker and use as much of the mixture as you would use normal salt. You'll find, to your surprise, that this makes your food taste as salty as usual, but doesn't raise your blood pressure. Diabetics can do the same thing by dissolving sugar in water, and use this super-diluted solution to sweeten drinks, etc.

The "trick" to making this work is that the mixing should be done *mindfully*, imagining the taste of the salt (or sugar) as you mix. You can put a *little* bit of salt or sugar in your mouth as you do this, to help you mentally capture the right taste as you mix. There should be nothing hurried about the mixing – in fact, it is best to only do one dilution at a time (per day), because while you don't need total concentration on what you're doing, you can't let your mind be wandering all over the place either. You have to give the taste of salt (or sugar) as much attention while you mix as you give to your sense of touch when you're having sex. How long you mix and how many dilutions you make, is up to you. Use your own intuition. When you get tired, or feel like that's good enough, then stop. The end product won't taste like salt if you eat it straight, but it should make foods you sprinkle it on taste salty enough for your taste (and it should work for other people too). If it doesn't, then you didn't take enough time in your mixing. Throw that batch out and do it again, but this time with more patience.

It's best to eat lots of salads. Lots of things can be mixed together in salads because raw vegetables, even after being picked and cut up into salad, are still alive and lively and enjoy the company of other vegetables. But things that are being cooked basically want to be left alone, and to throw a lot of condiments or other ingredients into them at such a time is disrespectful. No dressing is needed on salads, but if you prefer one it is best to use olive oil and fresh lemon juice stored in separate decanters and poured over the salad at the table. Sprouts of all sorts are an excellent food, not only from a nutritional point of view, but because their light fiber energy has all the vibrancy, impetuosity, and joie de vivre of youth (compared to the more experienced and mellow energy of e.g. a broccoli).

Eat slowly, chewing well. Don't drink during meals (half an hour before a meal and two hours afterwards). It is better to eat small quantities of food like snacks during the day rather than three big, heavy meals (but time and schedule constraints may prohibit this).

You should fast at least once a week, preferably on the same day each week. Rest that day and try to get off by yourself in nature. Whenever you get too upset, a fast is called for. When you feel out of kilter you should stop eating. Three- and seven-day fasts are good several times per year. Truly, Thanksgiving should be celebrated by fasting rather than by gorging until stuffed; that would make people truly thankful.

Gardening Questions and Answers

The time when humankind decided to move from silent knowledge to reason was the same time it moved from hunting and gathering to agriculture. Agriculture was not undertaken because big game had died off, or any such reason, but rather because humanity wanted to experiment with thinking, social organization, etc. The human and grain gods made a deal at that point to help each other out. A similar deal was struck with e.g. the bovine god. Cows, in return for the loss of a certain measure of freedom (reduction to the status of property, having their children taken away from them, etc.), received in return freedom from random predators and the condition of something to be protected and defended by some pretty intense little monkey-like creatures.

Similarly, the way back to silent knowledge is through hunting. However it is possible to apply much silent knowledge to the practice of agriculture – hence these lessons. What follows are some samples of notes I've channeled regarding agriculture.

Q: How should I control insects and diseases in my garden?

A: Put three pieces of copal (or any acrid incense, such as patchouli) in your censer, and waft the smoke towards each infected plant as you walk down the row. At the same time, ask the afflicting agent to please leave your plants alone because you need them. You should feel as though the incense smoke is carrying your thought towards the plants. It's a good idea to leave a plant or two (maybe the one or ones at the end of each row, so you remember) for the insects or disease. Don't waft incense at these plants. Tell the insects or disease that these plants are for them. Be nice about it. Be sincere. Mean what you say. Say it out loud.

Frankincense (or any light, happy incense such as sandalwood) is used to prevent disease and insect infestations (where copal is used to cure infected plants). Waft the incense towards each plant in turn, sending that plant the wish that it will grow well and be fruitful. It is best to be naked when you do this (or any gardening), simply because that is the most joyous way of doing it. This means gardening at night, in the moonlight, so the neighbors won't see you.

Q: Will this method work for anyone?

A: It will work for anyone who believes in it and means what they are telling the animals or plants. Actually, the incense is completely unnecessary. That's just for you, to help you pay attention to what you're doing and give you the sense that you're doing something "magical". It's the thoughts and desires that you have and express that are the gist of the matter.

Q: What do I do about gophers?

A: Dig out the gophers' burrow and put a trap in it, to trap one gopher. It must be a trap which catches the gopher alive and unhurt. Take the captured gopher to a cage in a dark, protected place, and give it food and water every day. Talk to it gently when you bring its food and water. Tell it you won't hurt it – in fact, you'll let it go – but it must take a message back to its brothers.

Keep this up (talking gently to the gopher when you feed it) until you have gained its trust. This doesn't mean friendship or petting it, but rather until it knows it has nothing to fear from you. How long this takes will depend upon you and the gopher. When you sense that it is calm (unthreatened) in your presence, tell it that it and all its brother gophers must leave your garden and orchard. Appoint some other place on your land where you don't care if there are gophers, and tell the captured gopher that it and its fellows must move to this other place. If you want to sweeten the deal, promise that you'll plant sweet potatoes or beets at this other place just for them. If you do make a promise like this, you must keep it.

Then, after repeating this message to the captured gopher for some days (until you feel it has "understood"), release the gopher back into its tunnel, bidding it to take this message to its fellows.

This same method will work for cutter ants. Stand over their trail while they are working (it won't work if they can't hear you), and ask them to please find food in some other direction, as you need these trees yourself. Be polite. One such treatment should be enough. If it isn't, repeat the next day, but ask them why they didn't obey you the first time. Write down their answer as you are writing this (by automatic writing). You may have to work out some sort of compromise or make a deal with them.

Q: What about planting our own bananas?

A: Bananas are your angels. Anything coming from them is love – love – love, from the tenderness of young leaves to happy, humorous browning splotched leaves, to the spongey, thick, soggy stems. And the tall, older leaves. They all fully participate in love. Of all plants, these will give and receive love more than any other. Their blessings come down with a gentle, steady flow of love droplets.

This is why you must always have bananas growing close to wherever you live (preferably fruiting, not ornamental, varieties). If you ever go North at least grow one as a pot plant. There is no greater gift you can give to those in the North than these plants.

Q: What about Biodynamic techniques?

A: Yes. Steiner's techniques as enunciated in his lectures on agriculture are excellent. He was a genius, and in touch with the spirit keepers of agricultural knowledge (as were also the founders of Findhorn). However, Steiner's techniques are no more valid than the ones we are channeling to you; they are merely more detailed, more specific, and more complex. A professional farmer would do well following Steiner. And anyone who elects to use Steiner's methods would do better making the formulations themselves rather than buying them ready-made. The important thing is to put one's own, personal vibration into the soil and plants. Stirring plain water – joyously – for hours and then spraying it on the soil or plants is better than using store-bought formulations and not stirring long enough, or stirring without a joyous heart. Everything you do in agriculture should be done with joy, or else you are better off not doing it at all. Fortunately agriculture is innately a joyous occupation, so this isn't hard to do.

Q: Steiner had a lot of wacky techniques for dealing with weeds, insects, and disease; but even Pfeiffer and his other followers admit they don't work. Why not?

A: Because they doubt they'd work. It is your (and Pfeiffer's) doubt that keeps these techniques from working. If you had no doubt whatsoever that they'd work, they'd work.

That's the only reason your materialistic world "works" – that when you turn on a TV, it turns on – is because you believe it. If you believed in these techniques with the same certainty that you believe turning a key in an ignition will start a car, then they would work.

Q: How should I graft?

A: As usual. However, fill the censer with frankincense (or sandalwood). Cense the tree from which the scions are to be taken. Tell it that you are sorry to hurt it, but that the twigs you are taking will become new little trees. Ask if this is okay.

Cense the scions with the wish that they take and prosper. Cense the rootstocks and apologize for hurting them, and tell them they will be getting new "heads" which are more productive, and that they will soon be living in the actual earth. If you feel that a particular scion or rootstock objects, then don't graft that one. It wouldn't take anyway. Then graft as usual, but as you do each graft talk to the stock and scion and wish them well, that they may join and prosper and be fruitful.

After grafting, run your hand gently up the rootstock and scion, and as you do so visualize in your mind's eye the graft taking and healing, the tree growing from a sapling to a young tree to a mature tree; and as your hand passes above the top of the scion, look up and see the mature tree full of fruit.

Then bend down and kiss the graft, with the wish that it will take and the tree prosper. Do this with true love and good feeling. And then commend the tree to the earth.

On Not Letting the S.O.B.'s Get You Down

The spiritual path would be a cinch if it weren't for the S.O.B.'s. Loving one's neighbor wouldn't be any problem if it weren't for the S.O.B.'s. And, unfortunately, the world is full of them. So at some point in our spiritual journey it behooves us to take a moment to try to figure out how to handle the S.O.B.'s.

Fundamentally there are only two ways of dealing with an S.O.B.: submission, or ruthlessness. Submission can take two forms – we can either cower and whimper in fear, or we can rage in anger. Either of these reactions says, "I accede to your game plan on your terms. I will allow you to bum me out. I will accept your self-hatred as my own." Both of these reactions are forms of self-pity, and permit the S.O.B.'s to actually suck our energy. As long as we react to them we are saying, "Here are the reins to my life. I'll permit you to decide how I'm going to feel."

Of course, we're making the latter statement any time we go to another person for validation or approval. But when we go for validation to someone whom we know is going to reject us (refuse to pity us when we whimper or to fear us when we rage) then we are actively collaborating in our own oppression. If we cleave to people who cause us grief, then obviously we're playing some sort of ego game ourselves.

Neither whimpering nor raging take responsibility for the realities of our situation. If the turkeys are oppressing us in the first place, they obviously aren't going to be moved to compassion by our pleas nor frightened by our anger. Neither whimpering nor raging can ever be intelligent strategies for dealing with S.O.B.'s They are just phony little acts we put on for ourselves to make us feel superior to our oppressors – more sensitive, more righteous, more justified in indulging our negativity – i.e. to try to force ourselves into their space rather than to eject them from ours.

To encroach upon other people's space means to deal with them in bad faith, to treat them as objects rather than as living, feeling people; even when (especially when) this is done in the name of "love" (to "help" them). To disrespect another person's feelings, to try to impose one's own feelings or viewpoint on another person, is literally a form of vampirism. It's a way unhappy people can alleviate their own unhappiness by forcing other people to bear their burden for them. Torturers and sadists do this quite consciously, deliberately, and shamelessly, getting an ego jolt from their victim's fear. But only true black magicians do it competently – they can actually extend their own lifespans by sucking other people's energy (this is explained in detail in my book *Thought Forms*). The point is that the everyday S.O.B.'s are not doing anything intrinsically different from what a vampire does, only they do it ineptly (unconsciously). Black magic is simply bad faith – making other people feel bad: feeling superior to them, sliming on them, criticizing them, picking at them, making them feel fearful, or angry, or guilty. It can only be defeated by a complete refusal to react.

Turning the other cheek is not an act of submission, but of defiance (ruthlessness). It is not an act of supine acquiescence to another person's self-hatred, but rather is saying, "I acknowledge that you have the upper hand; but I am not afraid of you, nor will I play the game by your rules. I refuse to accept ownership of your self-hatred."

We only put up with other people in our space as long as we're willing to put up with something ugly inside ourselves. When we are ready to make a change – to cast the ugliness out of ourselves, then either we hurl the S.O.B.'s out of our space, or else they know it's time to retire on their own hook. If we analyze the content of our images / fantasies about the S.O.B.'s, we'll observe that in every case the intent is an attempt to make the S.O.B.'s feel bad – the same thing the S.O.B.'s do to us. To break out of this cycle someone (presumably us) has to stop feeling bad, and stop trying to make the other person feel bad.

Ruthlessness means gently but firmly ejecting other people from our space. It doesn't mean being cruel or closed-hearted, which would entail encroaching upon their space, but it does mean being unyielding, pitiless. It means holding our own feelings inside instead of hurling them back at our oppressor.

Being ruthless also means doing whatever is possible to remedy the situation. This sounds rather obvious, but how often in life do we prefer to suffer the slings and arrows of outrageous fortune rather than take arms against a sea of troubles, and by opposing end them? If a situation is clearly impossible, then we've got to grin and bear it. If a guy's standing there with a gun leveled at us, there isn't much we can do.

But often we grin and bear it out of a self-hatred agenda of our own. If we're too timid to speak up or act up in order to change an unbearable situation, then we're acceding to our own oppression and seeking self-pity in the situation. Other people can't get into our space unless we let them in. They can most certainly hurt us, but they can't put a crimp in our space, bend our feelings around, force their unhappiness on us, without our connivance. Unless our oppressor holds over us the power of instant life or death with no possibility of escape, then there's surely *something* we can do to alleviate our plight besides helplessly wringing our hands and bemoaning our fate.

If you are not comfortable in a relationship, then decide what changes could be made so that you *are* comfortable, and ask the other person nicely to please make that adjustment. And if they ignore you or shoot you down, then cut the relationship off sharply right there. Turn around, walk away, shake off the dust of your feet, and don't look back. Of course, the other person may object or have changes that he or she wants to make. In that case you work it out in good faith together until you reach an accord you can both live and feel comfortable with. But if he or she refuses to act in good faith, then cut them off.

But when there's nothing more humanly possible which we can do to ameliorate the situation and get the S.O.B. off our case, then we've got to take it. And by "take it" is meant *take it* – not hurl our anger and frustration back in the S.O.B.'s face; not take it out on other people in our environment such as our children, spouse, employees; not whine and complain to other people about our plight; but rather absorb the S.O.B.'s bad vibes without reacting to them – just hold our own feelings in and be as joyous as we can manage.

All anger is self-anger; all hatred is self-hatred. If you are angry at someone it is because you are angry at yourself for permitting yourself to be bent out of shape by this person. If a three-year-old screams at you, "I hate you!", you laugh it off, right? You don't take it to heart. But when a grown-up does it, you do. That's you, buddy, not them. That's your decision (to let them bend you out of shape). To truly love yourself is to love someone who is rejecting you in spite of what they're doing – just as you would do with a three-year-old: not take that rejection personally (to heart), not let that rejection supplant your love for yourself, not let that person's rejection of you become your rejection of yourself (by caring what that person does or doesn't do).

Ruthlessness also means seriously considering S.O.B.s' criticisms of us for their information value. This is being ruthless with oneself. Even if the S.O.B.'s are just putting us down gratuitously, quite often the things they say about us are quite true. Moreover, these things are often things which our good friends won't tell us, either because they overlook them or because they've learned to accept them. The only really objective information about ourselves that we get comes from our enemies.

If what the S.O.B.'s think and say about us is blatant, out-and-out lies, then what's that got to do with us? Why even bother about it? On the other hand, if we feel put out about what they think or say about us, then that can only be if on some level or other we know that they are right. If we take the S.O.B.s' actions personally, as if they applied to us, that can only mean that they *do* apply to us. Otherwise we'd realize that the S.O.B.s' actions are just a manifestation of their self-hatred, and feel sorry for them, instead of being affronted and feeling ourselves to be better than them.

Maybe the S.O.B.s' criticism of us is just a mote in our eye compared to the beam in theirs. But every S.O.B. has as much right to his or her feelings as we have to ours. Even if their feelings about us are unjustified hatred of us and a desire to cause us pain, they have a right to have whatever feelings they want. Giving other people space means leaving them alone in their self-hatred – not trying to change them, help them, convince them, indulge them, or submit to them out of fear or guilt. Being open with people doesn't mean being honest, if honesty isn't going to be understood or appreciated. To go to our oppressors saying (on any level), "You have no right to feel about me or to treat me the way you do" is to deny them their space, to try to impose our point of view on them, which is always an ineffectual enterprise, but doubly so when the other person has the whip hand. Presumably our oppressors didn't pick on us at random – presumably they think they have some score or other to settle from another lifetime or reality – and if we could see what we did to them in that lifetime, it might help us to understand why they feel compelled to pester or injure us in this one.

If someone is being hateful to us, there must be something hateful within us that they are seeing. That hatefulness may stem from another lifetime, but even so, it is within us. To pretend that it isn't, to disavow responsibility for our own karma, is a hateful thing to do. Effects don't arise without a cause. The S.O.B. is saying to us, "I see something hateful in you." To reply, "No there isn't. You're imagining things." is being extremely disrespectful of his or her feelings. To assume that our judgment is superior to theirs (that we are more important than them) is a hateful thing to do. To make excuses for what we've done in other lifetimes is still making excuses for ourselves.

And besides, most of the time what S.O.B.'s see in us is not just something that happened in another lifetime; they're seeing something that's going on right now. If the S.O.B.'s appear hateful in our eyes, then what we're seeing is the reflection of our own hatefulness; otherwise we'd feel sorry for them.

If there is someone who is oppressing us, then we must look sharply about: there is someone whom we are oppressing in precisely the same fashion. An oppressor can only cause us pain by pressing on our self-importance; and if we've got self-importance, there must be someone we are pressing on with it. It cannot happen that someone could be deep in our space unless we are at the same time deep in someone else's space. We must pay very careful attention to this point, because unless we ourselves can see how and with whom we are oppressing other people, we'll never understand the lesson which the S.O.B. who is oppressing us is there to show us. We can't get the guy in front of us to get off our foot until we get off the foot of the guy in back of us.

To try to get rid of the S.O.B.s' bad vibes by sloughing them off on other people is to join the S.O.B.'s in their game plan. Somebody at some time laid all those bad vibes on the S.O.B.'s, and they try to get rid of them by passing them on to us. And if we do the same thing – try to pass them off onto other people – then we're hooking ourselves into a conveyer belt of bad vibes, doing our small part to destroy the earth. Whereas if we absorb the bad vibes by holding them in instead of reacting to them or hurling them at other people, then we're doing our small part to heal the earth. The buck has to stop somewhere; somewhere, at some time, someone has to take responsibility for cleaning up all the dreck in the world; and the bad vibes which those S.O.B.'s are laying on us is our share of the mess that has to be cleaned up.

To try to avoid S.O.B.s' bad vibes by hurling them back at them or by laying them in turn on other people is to duck out of our personal responsibility to the universe. Putting up with those S.O.B.'s is the precise reason why we were put on the earth at this time. Bearing up under their attacks on our self-importance (rather than defending our self-importance from attack) is the only way to wear our self-importance down and eradicate it. Feeling the heat of the S.O.B.s' bad vibes without surrendering our own inner peace is our only path to enlightenment; it's the only important and worthwhile task in our lives at this moment.

Basically our problem is that we are never taught how to relate to other people – to respect their space and our own. Everyday society – the bulk of our interactions with other people – consists of everybody rubbing their own self-importance and self-hatred in everybody else's faces. We're taught to relate to other people the same way we're taught to relate to bugs who bite us: either we sit there letting them suck us, or else we swat them. We don't know how to have a relationship with people any more than we know how to relate to bugs. We could talk to the bugs and ask them nicely to please stop biting us; and maybe they'd even listen and leave us alone. And if they don't, we can gently but firmly shoo them away.

We treat other people just like bugs. We either let them suck us (which is indulging them, but we mistakenly believe it is loving them or being patient with them), or else we swat them. We don't take responsibility for there being a relationship there – an assumption that we can coexist rather than become locked into winning or losing.

Loving one's enemies doesn't mean kissing and slobbering over them; it just means being pleasant and courteous to them, treating them in the same way that we would prefer they treated us, being joyous and happy in spite of them. It means not being offended by the S.O.B.'s, not depersonalizing them and turning them into objects – excuses for our own self-hatred and self-pity. Loving the S.O.B.'s means loving oneself in the presence of the S.O.B.'s – giving the S.O.B.'s a role model of joy, instead of a reflection of their own anger and uptightness.

In everyday society most of what's really going on is covered up by a mountain of lies, pretense, and hypocrisy. So much bad faith goes by the name of "love"; it seems that the people who profess to love us the most are always the ones who hurt us the most. William Faulkner's novels have a good sense of this emotional undercurrent level of everyday society – the contrast between what is apparently going on on the surface, and what is really going on underneath. In Faulkner's novels the S.O.B.'s like Popeye, Flem, and Christmas are shown for what they really are: sad, confused people who are starving for love, but who feel so unworthy of it that they can only cry out (through their behavior), "Oh, hate me! Reject me! I am so ugly and hateful, and I need your anger and fear to validate my self-hatred!"

The only way we can ever beat the S.O.B.'s at their own game is to love them anyway.

Photograph Gazing

Most of us don't realize the extent to which our social training distorts our very senses. In our society we are taught to repress our true feelings and to engage our complete attention in an interminable inner dialogue every minute we are awake, which effectively blocks our ability to perceive the world outside ourselves. Occasionally we emerge from the constant babble to cast a glance about to check out where we are and what we're doing; but then we fall back into our familiar daydreams of glory and vindication.

Even when we are face-to-face with other people, we don't actually *see* them most of the time, but only gloss over them. We are only *seeing* other people when we are looking them directly in the eye and paying attention to them (feeling with them).

Developing your psychic vision (and your other psychic abilities) is really just a matter of paying attention to the little things going on around you. Most people miss out on the magic of life because they have all their attention focused on the hurly-burly hustle-bustle. To develop your psychic abilities you have to slow down a bit and pay attention to the little, peripheral details rather than the big-screen image; and also not focus directly on things, but rather look out of the corner of your eye at them (as it were). All gazing exercises begin by relaxing your gaze by lightly crossing your eyes, in order to create a double image.

In order to recondition the way in which you look at the world, it is first necessary to decondition it. You reverse your social training by returning to seeing what your eyes actually *are* seeing: namely, two images. Adults take it completely for granted that they only see a single image with their two eyes; but they had to learn how to do this. A newborn sees two images, and it takes some time for babies to learn how to ignore (screen out) this fact, so as to blend the two images into one. Adults get so used to doing this that they don't even realize how much effort they are putting out to maintain this focus every second. If you have ever been stinking drunk, then you know how difficult it is to focus your eyes in that state. This same strenuous effort – forcing the two images together (or better said, forgetting that there are two images being seen) – is exactly what newborns have to learn how to do, but without even the memory of focused vision to guide them.

Usually a baby accomplishes this tour de force at about two months of age, when he or she begins smiling at people. Before that time the infant had to integrate two, less-focused visual images of the person. And, as this photograph gazing exercise will show, it is not readily apparent to an infant that the two images which he or she is seeing reference the same person, inasmuch as the two images can appear quite different, and have very different feelings to them (e.g. one can appear friendly, but the other one quite scary, as in the Joseph Stalin photograph below). So it takes the infant a while to realize that there is only one person there that he or she is seeing; and that there is only one witness there seeing that person (rather than two).

It is in fact your socially-conditioned ability to create just one visual scene out of two which props up your sense of there being a single, unified ego (a "you" to whom things are happening). To newborns there are two witnesses, not one; and as a result newborns have little sense of possessing a self at center – of there being a unified "me" there (this is actually a very important philosophical point, which is discussed in my book *Thought Forms*).

This is in fact what your two eyes are seeing all the time – two images. This is how newborns see the world. It was your social training (in your first few months of life) which taught you how to "blend" these two images into one scene. The effort involved in maintaining this moment-to-moment focus on one image is actually quite a strain; but you (like all adults) have become so accustomed to the effort involved that you don't realize how unnatural and uncomfortable it is, and how much visual information you lose in the process. By relaxing your gaze and returning your attention to the actual scene (double image) which is presenting itself to your field of vision, your eyes are freed up to grasp subtle nuances lost in single-image vision.

Photograph gazing is a simple exercise you can use to enhance your ability to feel with other people – to truly see them, rather than look mindlessly their way. When you look at a photograph in the usual way, you are looking at it with your concepts – i.e., standing apart from it. But when you gaze at a photograph, you are seeing it with your feelings, and so in a sense you become a part of the scene.

Candid photos, particularly photos in which the subject is in the throes of emotion, are usually more interesting and revealing than posed photographs, such as the photographs used to illustrate this essay. This is because in portraits the subjects have the opportunity to compose themselves, to put on a mask, whereas in candid photos the subjects are caught in the act, as it were. There's usually less difference between the left and right sides in posed photos than in candid photos.

Take a photograph of a person's face. I find it easiest to use a full or three-quarter face photograph in which the face is between 1½ and 2½ inches high; but you can use a magnifying glass with snapshots. You can also use a real, live person's face, but you'd better explain what you're doing first or they'll think you're nuts (once you've explained then they'll *know* you're nuts).

Hold the photograph a few inches from your eyes so that the image splits in two. Some people prefer to hold the photograph further away and cross their eyes lightly to produce the two images; with large photographs or with real, live people's faces, you have to cross your eyes to produce the two images. It may take a little adjustment until you can hold the two images on a neutral background simultaneously. If you feel too stiff, you can loosen yourself up by blinking. If other faces or background in the photograph interfere with the images, cover them with a piece of paper. Cover anything which distracts you.

If crossing your eyes blurs the images, don't worry about it: what you are after here are feelings rather than visual details. That's why single-image vision evolved in the first place – to obtain that greater clarity and visual detail (particularly the enhanced sensitivity to motion, useful to predatory animals such as humans) which are available via parallax. But in gazing exercises, how the scene feels is more important than what it looks like, so it's okay if the two images look a bit fuzzy.

Keeping the images split, give your attention first to one, then to the other of the two images. You will begin to notice that the two images are not the same – that the general appearance of the image, and even the expression on the subject's face, is different on the left and right sides. The difference can be quite startling: when I gaze at photographs of myself as a child, for example, no matter if on the left side I am smiling or laughing, on the right I am invariably crying or angry. Similarly, in most photographs of my father (especially in his last years), even when he appears jolly on the left, he is usually seen to be in great pain and agony on the right.

The image which appears on the left (i.e., which is seen with your right eye) shows the subject's outer personality – the self that he or she is consciously acknowledging and presenting to the world (at the time the photograph was taken). The image which appears on the right (i.e., which is seen with your left eye) shows the subject's inner personality – his or her true feelings at the time of the photograph.

First see if one or the other image is more distinct.

Gertrude Stein

When the right hand image is sharper, clearer, larger, or more colorful (if a color photograph) than the left hand image, this means that the subject is deeper than is apparent, or is feeling feelings which he or she is not showing openly. For example, in the photo of Gertrude Stein, The left side seems flat, two-dimensional, stand-offish. The left looks severe and masculine; also sadder and more tired – it's her predominant side. The right side seems wiser, more amused or ironic about life; also more kindly, motherly, feminine. On the right she is looking directly at the camera, but on the left she's gazing abstractedly past it.

F. Scott Fitzgerald

In the photo of F. Scott Fitzgerald, the left image seems a bit larger and sharper, but also stiff and nondescript, as though he's hiding his real self or keeping his real feelings under wraps. The right image is smaller and darker, but also more mischievous – more human and humorous – and more piercing in its gaze.

It must be emphasized that everyone gazes at photographs somewhat differently, and the way in which I happen to see things is not necessarily the way you will see them. Obviously there is something of a Rorschach blot test about this exercise; but as is also the case with Rorschach blots, people do tend to see much the same things. There is no right or wrong way to do it – everyone has to figure it out for themselves. For me, the two images are perceived differently; but for some people the feeling occurs in the middle of the two images (the images themselves are less important). The only thing that matters is to relax your eyes while keeping your attention focused.

The way I do this exercise, the left hand image reveals what the subject is trying to project consciously (the public self), whereas the right hand image reveals what he or she is really feeling inside. However, for some people it is the reverse. The way I see things, in the photo of Tallulah Bankhead she appears aloof, detached and indifferent on the left side – supercilious or

Tallulah Bankhead

dubious. She's posing here – she seems doll-like, fake, as though she is a porcelain statue. On the right she seems happier, warm and knowing, even a bit seductive. It's like a before and after photo: on the left she's made-up, whereas on the right she's more natural and human.

Nikolai Lenin

It is rare to encounter a subject who appears identical in both images. This indicates that the person is well-integrated, they know their inner feelings and express them openly (at least at the moment the photograph was taken). The person is neither repressing him or herself, nor pretending to be something they're not. For example, in the photo of Nikolai Lenin there's not a great deal of difference between the two sides, but he doesn't look happy on either side when split, even though unsplit he seems cheerful. The left side is a bit clearer, stronger, and harder than the right side: The left side is awake, whereas the right side has droopy eyelids and looks half asleep; the left side looks like it's quit having feelings, whereas the right side is tired of dealing with life.

After determining which image is more distinct, you must feel the two images, pick up the mood or attitude being expressed on each side. The difference between the two images does a have a visual basis, but it's more a matter of feeling than of sensory input. The image which is clearer or larger is also usually the one that feels the most alive and human, but not always. For example, in the photo of Joseph Stalin, The left side is fuzzier, shadier, less defined: he seems vaguely amused. The left side is more human – you could probably talk to this fellow. On the other hand, the right side is sharper, more

Joseph Stalin

dominant and harsh. On the right he looks truly evil and scary – you wouldn't want to face this guy if you could avoid it, much less cross him.

Once you have mastered the basic technique (which shouldn't take much more than ten minutes), you should employ it to gaze at photographs of your acquaintances and friends. You may be surprised to find that some people you consider your friends and allies are actually quite superficial or even predatory when split or seen on the right. It's a good idea not to be too trusting or naïve in your dealings with such people.

Salvador Dali   Man Ray

For example, in the photo of Salvador Dali, the left hand image is clearer and lighter. It seems stiff or mannequin-like, with something of a frightened, shell-shocked expression. On the right he seems warmer and more human, if a bit perplexed; he's more "there" on the right than on the left. When you split the image you can clearly see that he's faking it – putting on an act for the camera. Man Ray in the same photo seems serious or sad on the left side: aggressive, hard-edge, and unyielding, as if he's holding himself back or in. On the right side he is softer, more relaxed, introspective and pensive. He looks older and tireder on the left side than on the right, and also more withdrawn.

The object of this exercise is to get beyond your customary images to your true feelings about the people you know; to *feel* with them instead of becoming entangled in your own concepts of them. When you gaze at photos you may find that some of the people you dislike or consider your enemies are actually in pain on the right, and you might soften your attitude towards these people accordingly. For example, in the photo of Diego Rivera, the left side seems stronger and more forceful, like he is bracing himself for something. A stronger left than right side indicates a person who is playing a role or who is projecting a false image (at least at the moment the photo was taken). Diego Rivera's left side has a ready-for-anything attitude, with a crazed look, as if his eyes are about to roll back into his head in anger. The right side is more faded; also sadder, as if he's trying to hold back tears. On the left he is thinking his own thoughts, whereas on the right he isn't thinking at all – he's just contemplating.

Diego Rivera

The Mona Lisa's famous enigmatic smile can be deconstructed with this technique: on the left she has a beatific, abstracted, far-away expression – as if she were immersed in otherworldly concerns. She seems sad and wise, and a bit older, on the left. On her right side she is warmer, has more energy and sparkle, is more humorous and knowing (like a strumpet tipping a potential customer a wink).

Photograph gazing is not true gazing, but it is a good preliminary exercise for true gazing, scrying, seeing auras, and other visual psychic techniques. Gazing is a technique which can provide a doorway to astral projection, by entering directly into the gazing scene. To gaze, cross your eyes lightly and look at things which are close to you (not far away). To begin with, look at little things very closely. Scrutinize small things on the ground, or the bark of a tree up close. You shouldn't cross your eyes too tightly. It has to be a really loose and relaxed lack of focus. It's not a fuzziness per se, but a double image, and relaxed. In all gazing, the feeling is more important than the vision. Don't stare at the thing you're looking at. Glance at it and away and back again; or just to the side of it, as you do to see things at night. You don't look directly at things unless they are very solid-looking and are trying to show you something. That is to say, if they are trying to capture your attention. If you are accustomed to praying to an image (e.g. of Jesus, Mary, Krishna, Buddha), try to gaze at the image during prayer; you might be surprised by how well this facilitates true heart contact with the spirit of the image (brings the image to life).

One final point: unless it is absolutely necessary (e.g. for a passport or driver's license), it's best not to permit yourself to be photographed or videoed. As this exercise shows, the subject of a photograph leaves a little piece of him or herself in that photo; and it's a good rule of thumb in life not to strew pieces of yourself here and there purposelessly (I was trying to follow this dictum, but my guides – who channeled this set of magical training manuals to me – want them to be disseminated widely; and in the business of peddling New Age spiritual books that requires publishing cheesey smiling photographs of oneself on all of one's books and articles. So my guides told me to do that. At least, I picked a photo in which I'm not smiling).

Kidraising for Fun and Profit

It isn't all that hard to be a good parent. We all *want* to be good parents; we all *try* to be good parents; so with that motivation we're bound to succeed. Being a good parent is simply a matter of: 1) following our own hearts, and 2) ignoring everything society has taught us about childraising.

Fundamentally, it's not our job as parents to teach our kids how to get along in society – to worry about their achievements or how well they're doing socially – much less to chastise them for not "measuring up". Society has its Gestapo of teachers, coaches, clergymen, scout leaders, etc. – not to mention the pressure of peers, advertisers, and the media – to whip kids into line, to teach them to be "good citizens" and "team players", to "fit in" and "belong". So kids don't need more of that crap when they get home.

What kids need from their parents is *love*. They don't need criticism, blame, or guilt; they don't need unfavorable comparisons with other kids; they don't need to be belittled or patronized, or to be treated rudely because their parent had a bad day at work.

When our kids come home with a lousy report card, or when they've committed some other atrocity against society, do we chastise them and make them feel bad; or do we commiserate with them and try to make them feel good? They already feel bad at having transgressed society's expectations (even if they feign defiance). Therefore, to clamp down on them, to try to impose our will on them, is not going to help them any; and if they have any gumption at all, some day they'll spit it all back in our faces.

Babies do not come into this world grumpy and truculent and spoiling for a fight. Babies come into this world too spaced-out and vulnerable to be pugnacious. Therefore, if there is anger and fighting going on in a parent-child relationship, then it is logical to assume that the parent is 100% to blame for the situation.

Parents are confused, they are cowed and daunted by the sanctions society has in place if they fail in their role as taskmasters. Parents have to understand that it's *okay* if their kids are failing their grade or getting into fights or doing drugs or are unmarried and pregnant. If the kids are doing antisocial things or inviting dire consequences by their behavior, then obviously they're unhappy and out of kilter with their environment. It's a parent's duty then to say, "Hey, what's bugging you?" rather then "Shape up or ship out!" And if they don't want to talk to you, then you leave them alone. You give them space, respect their feelings and their right to make their own decisions.

Parents have to stop worrying about how their kids' behavior and achievements reflect back on them. Who cares what the teachers and the neighbors think? *Our kids' feelings are more important.* It's not a question of taking sides with the kids, but rather entails seeing things from the kids' point of view. It's not so much a matter of standing up for the kids, as standing by them. The teacher has the whole system backing him or her up; surely the kids deserve an impartial advocate, even if they're guilty as hell.

Society drives a wedge of guilt into the parent-child relationship even before the kids are born. The common fear (particularly with a first baby) that our kid might be born crippled or handicapped or something is actually fear that we won't be able to love the baby if it doesn't fulfill society's expectations.

Society puts a lot of heavy guilt trips on parents to make them feel ashamed of their kids ("Have you heard what Sarah's boy has done now?"); and parents pass those same guilt and shame trips on to their kids ("You have failed me, son."). Parents have to be reassured that no matter how their kids turn out, it doesn't mean that they failed as parents. Even if the kids turn out to be like Heliogabalus, if the parents gave them true love, then they did their job well. Even if the kids are truly weird or nasty – even if they masturbate publicly or torch the neighbor's cats – that is not the parents' fault, responsibility, or problem. It's the *kids'* problem.

It is not the parents' job to mold kids' characters or guide their development; to see that they have all the advantages or to teach them how to compete and succeed. The parents' only job is to love their kids, to be able to say to them, "Well, you certainly screwed up there, but don't take it to heart. You learned a lesson, you'll go on living and breathing, etc. etc." – whatever the kids need to hear at that moment to cheer up, to recover their sense of self-worth. That's what kids need from their parents, and it's the only thing they need – ultimate acceptance, no matter what they've done. And it's the parents' job to supply this.

We're not talking about indulging kids, letting them run rampant. In a "normal" parent-child relationship, the kids are taught to fear the parents' disapproval. But there are some parents who reverse the usual roles, and fear their kids' disapproval. Usually these kids become real hellions and grow up drunk with power, with little respect for other people's space. We're not talking about switching approval / disapproval roles; we're talking about dispensing with approval / disapproval altogether. Approval is as damaging as disapproval. To say to a kid, "I love you because you fulfill my expectations and make other parents envy me." is as nasty a thing to say to a kid as, "I don't love you because you bring me no glory." To discipline our kids, all we have to do is say to them, "Hey, I don't like what you did there for these reasons …." Period. Say it once, calmly, as you would do with another adult. Don't hammer at the kids and wipe your bad vibes all over them.

We must be willing to apologize to our kids when we've overstepped ourselves and made them feel bad needlessly; and this doesn't mean a half-hearted, "Oh well, maybe I overreacted there, but still you shouldn't have … ." It means a full, complete cop: "Sorry. I guess I got on your case about nothing."

The way we can tell if we're blowing it is: if we feel annoyed or disappointed in our kids, then we're wrong. If we ever feel anything other than good about our kids, accepting of our kids, sympathetic to our kids, then we're wrong. If we can't feel good about our kids at all times, then we're blowing it. This is why raising kids is such a terrific spiritual reality check – it shows us precisely how far away we are from enlightenment.

The trick is to tell kids what they're doing wrong calmly and collectedly, without releasing a dart of anger, impatience, or annoyance. Of course, to be able to do this we have to have our own self-importance under control – to be light and detached (rather than to permit ourselves to be sucked into our kids' bad moods).

If parents were enlightened beings, perhaps then they would have a moral right to interfere in their kids' lives. If parents were exalted beings (as their kids believe them to be), maybe then their approval or disapproval would have value. But the fact is that parents don't have any more of a clue as to what's really going on than their kids do. The only guide they've got is what their own parents drummed into them: fear of disapproval.

We should act towards our kids exactly the same way that we wished our parents had done for us when we were kids. It's trite to say it, but inevitably, 100% of the time, when we are angry at our kids about something, what we are angry at is precisely what our parents used to get angry at us about.

From whom did we learn that this behavior (what our kid is doing) is unacceptable? Why does this behavior anger us? Not the ostensible reason – what we are telling ourselves and the kid – but rather the actual reason why we find such-and-such a behavior objectionable: what our kid is doing openly that our parents forced us to repress. See, we all tell ourselves that we're angry at our kids because of this or that very valid reason. We all have impeccably logical reasons why we must bend our kids out of shape; close our hearts to them by labeling their feelings "acceptable" or "unacceptable"; force them to knuckle under to us in exactly the same fashion that our parents forced us to knuckle under to them. We thereby pass our own anger at our parents for having forced us to knuckle under on to our kids, as if to say to our parents, "See, Mommy and Daddy! I forgive you for having closed your hearts to me and having put more importance on your images than on my true feelings – my need as a completely vulnerable infant for the greatest tenderness, delicacy, and respect – for I have done the same thing to my own children!" And so it goes: the torch of self-hatred is handed down from generation to generation. It only stops if we quit getting angry at our kids altogether, no matter what they do or don't do. This is not all that hard to do once we make the connection that in spite of all our wonderful logic and self-justification, all we're doing when we're angry with our kids is upholding that side of our own parents which we despised the most.

To a kid his parents are God incarnate. If a kid feels he can trust his parents, then later on he'll naturally trust in God. Another way of saying this is, upon becoming parents we take upon ourselves the mantle of Godhood willy-nilly. This is a very serious presumption and responsibility. Most of us blow it. But the point is, since we are masquerading as God, we should at least do a good job of faking it.

This means giving our kids 100% acceptance and forgiveness, no matter what they've done (just as God does for us). Check out how God deals with us: when we screw up, does God dramatically appear in a burning bush and give us hell? No, God doesn't do that; God leaves us alone to stew in our own juice and to figure things out for ourselves. To treat our kids like God treats us means not making them feel worse about themselves, but rather better, as if they were still worthwhile beings, worthy of salvation and redemption, no matter how sinful they may have been. It means not being angry with them but rather tender with them; feeling what they feel instead of trying to make them feel our feelings (agree with us).

Most parents have truly loving impulses; but society sends parents the wrong messages – it makes them feel guilty about being "weak" or "soft-hearted" or "spoiling" kids. Parents just have to know that feeling with their kids – withholding all negative judgment, criticism, and blame, is okay; that it's fine to be completely tender and sympathetic all the time; that it's not a sign of weakness to understand things from the kids' viewpoint.

When you get annoyed with your kids, think of this: if they were to die in the next moment, would you still give a damn about whatever you are angry at them about? Is that what you would want your last message to them to be – annoyance over some stupid triviality?

The next time you jump on your kids for something, think about how you would feel if they were to die in your arms in the next moment; and ask yourself if whatever you're on their case about is worth trashing the short time you will spend on this earth together.

The Secret of Effective Prayer

The secret of effective prayer is to pick a propitious astrological time to launch your prayers heavenward. When we pray to the Spirit for something, we're not telling it anything it doesn't already know; the Spirit knows what's in our hearts and minds. Our prayers are rather for our own benefit, to state unequivocally, before the Spirit, a certain intent. The Spirit neither gives nor withholds; the outward circumstances of our lives are wholly the product of our own karmic and emotional state. To change the outward circumstances of our lives, then, we must first change our inner state. We do this by making a definite, unalterable decision.

Why, then, is it necessary to use astrology to choose a time to launch a prayer? Well, if we are already lucky – in tune with our innermost desires and capable of reaching out and taking what we want from life with neither shame nor hesitation – then we don't need astrology. Lucky people are using astrology naturally; they have an inner clock which tells them when it's time to act or to refrain from action. However, most of us aren't so attuned to our own inner feelings and the ambient rhythms of the universe. Or rather, we *are*, but we deliberately (albeit unconsciously) choose unpropitious times to launch new projects, or to pray for what we want. Just ask any astrologer how often it's happened that a client has requested a propitious time to e.g. open a new business, or marry, or ask a favor, but when the time came the client wasn't able to use it. This is because the client (subconsciously) wanted to fail.

Many of us have subconscious agendas of unworthiness which contradict what we consciously tell ourselves we want. For example, we may be consciously telling ourselves that we want love, or health, or riches; but at any point that our conscious desires seem to be on the brink of being realized, we ourselves will do something to blow the opportunity and then later moan and complain about our bad luck.

When do we normally pray (ask the Spirit) for things? When we're feeling lousy and pitying ourselves, right? – i.e., at the worst possible astrological time. This guarantees that our prayers won't come true. Asking the Spirit for things at a poor time astrologically is a subconscious ploy to maintain our agendas of unworthiness intact.

There are two ways to overcome these subconscious agendas which hold us back from realizing our desires:

Commit ourselves to years of psychotherapy or other inner work to get to the root of our neurotic, self-defeating patterns, which invariably stem from childhood experiences and traumas, usually laid on us by our parents; or

Use astrology to bypass the hang-ups, to cut through the underlying feelings of unworthiness which make us seek self-pity rather than success, and to just get on with our lives. Nothing succeeds like success: we can spend years analyzing and agonizing why we're unlovable or poverty-stricken; or we can just go out and find someone to love us or make a bunch of money. The end result is the same, and astrology is the key that enables us to do this.

When making a wish or prayer it is best to attach the desire to a powerful current of universal energy. It's like the difference between talking normally and talking through a loudspeaker: by attaching a desire to a wave of ambient energy we magnify its power (increase the likelihood of its realization). This is the basis of animal and human sacrifice: when the Spirit descends for the soul of the sacrificial animal, the sorcerer attaches his own desires to it, and up they go. However, there are less drastic methods available for getting the same effect, and these are: praying on ephemeral phenomena, praying at propitious places, and praying at propitious times.

Ephemeral phenomena such as rainbows, falling stars, dust devils, gusts of wind, etc. are actually the best messengers for taking our prayers and wishes out into the universe because they spring to life for a moment, and then dissolve back into undifferentiated energy, taking our prayers with them. It is also possible to attach a prayer to a burning candle, as is done in many churches; or to flags or kites, as is done in the Orient; but ephemeral phenomena which we encounter by chance are far more powerful messengers, therefore we should be alert to seize these impromptu opportunities when they occur.

Praying at propitious places means using power spots such as shrines, mountaintops, pools and waterfalls, and the abodes of nature spirits. Churches (especially old churches; especially old churches built on sites of previous pagan worship) are often built on power spots. There are also certain trees which facilitate making prayers. To find such a tree, enter a woods, preferably during a lunar planetary hour, and walk in the direction your intuition dictates until you come to a tree which feels "right". Then make your prayer on the spot.

Praying at propitious times is a whole science in itself, known as electional astrology. There are basically three steps to choosing a propitious time to launch a prayer (or any enterprise): finding a proper day, finding a proper hour, and finding a proper moment. Of these, the proper hour is far and away the most important; so if you're pressed for time and need to launch a prayer in a hurry, or if you have no knowledge of astrology, you can skip steps 1 and 3 below and just make your prayer during a propitious hour. There are propitious hours for every activity several times each day.

The most important method which we are employing here is known as the Planetary Hours, which has historically been the main astrological technique used in magical operations such as charging talismans; and also is the main astrological technique recommended by the spiritual guardians of astrological knowledge for all sorts of elections. It is based upon an ancient Chaldean system of astrology which supposedly antedates even the zodiac of signs.

The reason why astrology (and magic generally) doesn't "work" as well nowadays as it did in the past is because it is peripheral to the central concerns of our society: very little energy is presently being focused in that direction. Warlike societies tend to be successful at war; commercial societies like ours tend to be successful at commerce; spiritual societies tend to be successful at spiritual endeavors; and magical societies tend to get magic to work quite well. Whatever a society (or an individual) has faith in is what it tends to manifest. Most of us have rationalist-materialistic or spiritual-materialistic backgrounds and hence have little native faith in magic or astrology: faith, like knowledge, is handed down from generation to generation, and our New Age generation is the first of the new magicians. It is necessary for us to plug away at magic on blind faith for a while until we eventually start seeing positive results, which is what builds real faith. However, we can take a faith short-cut by tuning in to existing wavelengths of knowledge: by using the Planetary Hours we are forging a link with the ancient magician astrologers and the spirits who guided them.

Let's look a the procedure step-by-step:

1) CHOOSING A PROPITIOUS DAY: First identify what it is you are praying for with the relevant planet (see Table of Planetary Rulerships). For example, if what you want is money, then you must look to the planet Jupiter. In an astrological ephemeris (most monthly astrology magazines include current ephemerides) scan ahead for a day when there is a good transiting aspect to Jupiter, and note the time when this aspect is exact. Don't forget to convert the time given in the ephemeris to clock time for your locality, taking Daylight Saving Time into account (if it's in effect).

Optimally, the other planet involved in the aspect should also be relevant to what you want: if you want a steady income and a sense of security, then try to find a good aspect between Jupiter and Saturn (permanence); if what you want is money so you can afford some luxuries and enjoyment, then try to find a good aspect between Jupiter and Venus; if you want money so you can get ahead in life, then try to find an aspect between Jupiter and the sun. Most of the time, unless you're willing to wait for some months, you will be circumscribed in what choices are available, so in a pinch you can always go with aspects to the moon, which every possible aspect with every planet every month. Only favorable aspects should be used (conjunctions, sextiles, and trines);

ignore unfavorable and minor aspects, and parallels of declination.

1)   CHOOSING A PROPITIOUS HOUR: To use Planetary Hours, download the free Planetary Hours calculator from: http://www.dearbrutus.com/body_planetaryhours.html. This is an Excel worksheet with complete instructions; however when you open it, it will ask if you want to disable the macros. Since it won't work with its macros disabled, click on "Enable Macros" (you may have to have previously reduced the Excel security protocol: Tools => Macro => Security => Low). If you prefer printed tables, see my book *Planetary Hours* which provides tables for latitudes from 58° North to 58° South.

Once you have located a propitious day, scan the Tables of Planetary Hours and locate an hour ruled by the planet in question (Jupiter in our example). If you're not paying attention to the transits, then just choose a Jupiter hour which is convenient for you. Otherwise, if the transiting aspect does not involve the moon then you can use any of the Jupiter hours which fall within twenty-four hours before the exact time of the aspect; and if the transiting aspect does involve the moon then you must use that one Jupiter hour which falls just before the exact time of the transit. If the aspect becomes exact during a Jupiter hour, then use the space in time between the beginning of the Jupiter hour and the exact time of the transit.

3)   CHOOSING A PROPITIOUS MOMENT: You can just go with the transiting aspect and planetary hour, but if you like doing calculations you can refine the technique further by using a table of houses to see whether a natal or transiting planet (preferably the one which rules whatever it is you are praying for) crosses any of the four angles during the planetary hour in question. However, this isn't all that important, so if you don't know how to do these calculations, don't worry about it.

Now that you have found a propitious time to launch your prayer, you must consider the form that your prayer will take. Write down ahead of time exactly what you want, so that you don't forget anything when the time comes. However, it's best not to be too specific in what you're asking for, such as to win the lottery, or to have such-and-such a person fall in love with you. It's best just to ask for wealth, or love from some unnamed person. Let the Spirit handle the details – it knows what it's doing.

If you have an accustomed mode of prayer, then just pray the way you usually do. If not, then you can adapt this formula to suit your own taste and needs: "Spirit – please bring me (whatever you are asking for), and please bring it to me really soon! Thank you!" It's important that you say "really soon", or else any contradictory subconscious agendas you may have will use this loophole to defeat the prayer. It's also important to say "thank you" at the end, as a reminder that the Spirit doesn't owe you (or anybody) anything. After all, the Spirit has given you life; after that anything else is gravy.

When the time draws near, prepare a little altar with something that symbolizes the Spirit above it (this can be a picture of Jesus if you're a Christian, or just a cut-out picture of an eye, or whatever symbolizes the Spirit for you). Put a stick of sweet-smelling incense on the altar, and a candle whose color symbolizes what you're asking for (green for money, pink for love, white for health or spiritual illumination, etc.). Also put on the altar objects which symbolize what you want (money if you want money; cut-out pictures of lovers if you want love; pictures of healthy, active people if you want health, etc.).

Just prior to the chosen time light the incense; and then, at the precise moment chosen for the prayer, light the candle. Then recite the prayer you've written down. It's okay to read it, but you should do this with feeling – true longing for whatever it is that you want. Picture in your mind's eye your prayer coming true as you pray, and let yourself feel all the joy you would feel if your prayer came true. Don't worry about whether you are doing it right; if you're doing it in good faith with true longing, then you're doing it right.

If you don't feel comfortable with all the ritual, you can dispense with it. The ritual is just for your own sake, to lend a sense of importance and ceremony to the occasion – not to impress the Spirit. The only things of importance are to pray with true longing, at a propitious time.

When you finish your prayer, leave the area and let the incense and candle burn down, and then dismantle the altar and dispose of what's left of the candle and incense by burying them. Once a prayer has been launched there's no need to repeat it unless you feel your own resolve weakening and want to strengthen it.

Sometimes astrologically guided prayer works so fast that the results are startling. At other times, when there are powerful contradictory subconscious agendas in place, it takes a while for your prayer to come true; but nonetheless you ought to be able to feel your prayer working right away in the sense of feeling your inner obstructions dissolving and your inner attitude changing. Be assured that prayer carried out in good faith always works, so don't waste prayer on anything frivolous, since then you're committed to it. Be sure you really want what you're praying for. Good luck!

Table of Planetary Rulerships

Note that the planetary hours can be used to find propitious times for commencing all sorts of activities, not just prayers; therefore the general uses of each planet are listed.

Sun ☀ Hours: General success and recognition; spiritual illumination; decisiveness, vitality; activities requiring courage or a mood of self-certainty – making big decisions, scheduling meetings for reaching decisions, giving speeches, launching new projects; seeking favors from father, husband, boss, authorities.

Venus ♀ Hours: Love; friendship; artistic and social success; enjoyable, sociable and aesthetic activities such as parties, social gatherings, recitals / exhibitions, weddings, visits, dating and seeking romance; planting ornamentals; buying gifts, clothing, luxuries; beauty treatments; seeking favors from women.

Mercury ☿ Hours: Success in studies / communications; children; making a good impression; routine activities and activities needing clear communications; teaching / learning; important business letters / phone calls; meetings to develop or communicate ideas; buying / selling; signing contracts; routine shopping, errands, travel; job applications / interviews; seeking favors from neighbors, co-workers.

Moon ☽ Hours: Health; home (buying home, moving); journeys / vacationing (time of leaving home or takeoff); activities remote in time or space – meditation, making reservations, finding lost objects or people; planting food crops; hiring employees; seeking favors from mother, wife, employees.

Saturn ♄ Hours: Discipline and patience; giving up bad habits; overcoming obstacles; success with difficult tasks or difficult people; projects of long duration – breaking ground, laying foundations; planting perennials; treating chronic illness; making repairs; seeking favors from older people (not relatives) or difficult people.

Jupiter ♃ Hours: Wisdom, optimism; money (borrowing / lending/ investing / earning / winning); activities necessitating enthusiasm; buying lottery tickets; seeking advice / consultation; settling disputes; seeking favors from grandparents, aunts and uncles, advisors (doctors, lawyers, accountants, astrologers).

Mars ♂ Hours: Courage, adventure; enforcing your will; success with drastic action (lawsuits, conflicts, going to war, surgery); sports, exercises; risk-taking; making complaints; firing employees; seeking favors of husband or boyfriend.

What's the Difference Between Faith and Fooling Yourself?

I once had a conversation with a woman who was thoroughly convinced that someday Jesus was going to bring her a "whole ton of money". I had occasion recently to question my spirit guides on this point, in connection with some money problems of my own.

B: What is the difference between faith and fooling yourself?

S: It's like the difference between indifference and apathy. Apathy is a thought form copy of indifference. With apathy, you squelch your true feelings; with indifference, you relax into your true feelings. You just RELAX. That is the difference between thought forms and true feelings – between fooling yourself and faith.

Faith means releasing your own plans and designs, your demands that the Spirit bring you money on your own terms and in your own time. Faith means emptying yourself of your own ego, and being willing to trust the Spirit, even if this means living on zero money.

B: But you could fool yourself into that one too.

S: Right, but in that case you wouldn't feel peaceful. Fooling yourself doesn't bring with it a sense of relief and release – the giving up of your own worries, the sense of urgency that your problems be solved. True release can only come when you give up grasping after a release. The grasping after a release is what keeps release at bay. Only when you give up looking for an exit, for an escape hatch; when you truly reach the end of your rope and have to let it go and drop into the abyss; can you feel true release – i.e., can you truly be released. Spiritual growth is basically just a matter of exhaustion.

What's the difference between faith and fooling yourself? Just the way they each feel. Faith is RELAXED, is not pushing to get anywhere, is not frantically seeking an exit. Fooling yourself is the belief that there *is* an exit – that if you somehow found the right button to push, God would deliver a miracle and save you. So you keep running around pushing every button in sight, and looking for more and more buttons to push, until you either run out of buttons or run out of energy to keep running around.

At that point you realize there is no exit. The Spirit isn't going to go out of its way to save you. It's at that moment that true faith becomes possible. True faith is peaceful, resigned, RELAXED. True faith isn't smug ("God is going to come through for me in such-and-such a manner."). That's why that woman was fooling herself in her hope that Jesus would bring her a whole lot of money.

B: Maybe he did.

S: Maybe he did. If she's a "lucky" person, she may even have gotten her wish answered, and she did win the lottery or something. But even if she got what she was wishing for, it probably just compounded her true problems.

True faith means not trying to dictate to the Spirit: "I want this and that and the other …" as if you were on Santa's knee asking him for toys. It means letting the Spirit bring you what is best for you – what your true feelings want, not what your thought forms want. Like that woman – what's she going to do with a fortune? Why not be content with a modest income? What she was trying to do was to dictate to the Spirit.

The point is that true faith does not depend upon the realization of a particular expectation. Believing that your thought form images – your miraculous escape from your present circumstances into some ideal fantasy world – will come true, is not faith. It's fooling yourself. This is what most people spend their entire lives doing. Most people live for the daydream that someday the object of their fondest fantasies will drop into their laps from heaven with no effort on their part.

True faith, by contrast, is faith that everything is unfolding as it should; so be patient. True faith is the conviction that things will happen precisely as you, in your inmost heart, need for them to happen; so go with the flow.

True faith is knowing that you can't control anything anyway, so you'd might as well quit worrying about it and just chill. Death will solve all your problems soon enough.

True faith, true trust in the Spirit, means shifting the burden of worrying about money over to the Spirit ... just giving up all that worry (importance). Faith is not so much the cessation of desire as it is the cessation of importance. When importance is gone, faith rushes in to fill the gap.

The Fire Speaks

Elsewhere I mention the importance of watching the candle flame carefully when you are casting a spell or making a prayer, in order to determine how the spell or prayer will go. I learned something of how to do this from my teacher don Abel Yat Saquib.

Kiché Mayan ceremonies such as those which don Abel performed take place at dawn around a fire, after an all-night vigil which alternates prayer with eating and socializing. The priest, chanting prayers and litanies to invoke the ancestors and Mayan deities all the while, begins by laying out a circle of decoratively arranged colored candles, copal pom incense, cigars, and herbs. The fire is then lit with prayers for the client (the person who has commissioned the ceremony). The fire is fed periodically thereafter with rum by the priest and with candles and incense by the participants, who throw them into the flames as offerings to the Mayan deities (or to petition something).

The fire in a *Kiché* Mayan ceremony is considered to be a living manifestation of *Ahau* (God), and when offerings are made to the fire during the ceremony, the flames are watched closely by the priest and participants for signs and messages from *Ahau*. The purpose of Mayan ceremonies is to please, propitiate, and thank *Ahau*; to create a balance between earth and heaven; and also to open a psychic channel – like a telephone or internet line – with *Ahau*, in order to obtain specific guidance, information, and healings for the participants. Most of this information is read from the behavior of the fire.

The Mayan priest observes the fire very closely all during the course of the ceremony. For example, at the beginning when the tower of candles in the middle of the fire is ignited and burns down, and the cigar in its center falls over, the direction in which it falls is taken to be a sign: if it falls to the east (the dawn), then this is good, the purpose of the ceremony will be fulfilled; but if it falls to the west (the night) then this isn't such a good omen.

The direction that the flames and smoke take in response to a prayer or healing are significant, as are sudden flares and bunches of sparks. Also, if the fire swirls around in a counterclockwise vortex, then this is a good omen; but if it swirls clockwise then it's a bad omen. If the fire divides in two then it's an omen that the present company will divide into factions and dispute. Now and again during the course of the ceremony the priest will dance around the fire and feed it with rum; or he will he stir the embers to raise the flames, all the while intently watching how the flames move, in order to see whether *Ahau* is pleased.

The omen basically is read for whichever participant is e.g. circling the fire at that moment; or receiving a healing; or whom the flames are pointing at. The interpretation depends upon the direction in which the flames tend during what portions of the ceremony. Bursts of flame or sparks, and whorls of flame, are interpreted as remarkable omens and interpreted according to how they act and what direction they take.

The interpretation of the omen also depends upon which one of the twenty *Chol Qij nagual's* portion of the ceremony it is (as explained in the article on *Mayan Ceremonies*, posted at : http://groups.yahoo.com/group/MagicalAlmanac/files/Mayan %20Calendar%20and%20Shamanism/), and whether the flame points in that *nagual's* direction or away from it. Each of the four cardinal directions rules five of the *naguals*. So if, for example, the flames tend to point to the south during the portion of the ceremony ruled by the *nagual Ajmak* (which is ruled by the south), then that is a good omen. If the flames point towards the north, then the opposite.

In terms of interpreting omens from the direction in which the ceremonial flames move, the east represents the upper world (the will of *Ahau*); the west the lower world (*Xibalba*, the consequences of karma whether from this life or due to ancestors, since much of what we would call "karma" the Maya ascribe to unresolved troubles due to ancestors); the north represents the past; and the south the future. Straight, vertical flames refer to the present, overseen by the Hearts of Heaven and the Earth. Movement of the flames from east to west is considered to be an omen relating to the spiritual life (a blessing from or need to propitiate *Ahau*); whereas movement of the flames from north to south relates to the material (human) life.

The Four Corners or directions of the Earth are an apotheosis of the first four humans (whose names are *Balam Kiché* in the East; *Balam Acab* in the West; *Iq' Balam* in the north; and *Majukutaj* in the South). The four directions also symbolize the human body. It is by watching the direction in which the flames tend when a given participant is being healed that the priest can read in what part of the body the participant needs healing, and how to go about it: East rules the head; West rules the legs; North rules the right arm and side (positive, strengthening energy); and South rules the left arm and side (negative, weakening energy). East relates to constitutional bodily weakness such as headaches, earaches; as well as nervous, circulatory, and back problems. West relates to health problems involving eyes, stomach and digestion, internal organs and spine. North indicates weakness in respiratory, digestion, and bones. South shows weakness in kidneys, liver, stomach, bones, skin, and feet.

Similarly, the behavior of the fire in response to petitions (e.g. for health, or economic prosperity) made during the course of the ceremony is a sign of whether and how the wish will be granted. Often during the course of the ceremony the priest will have certain individuals, or certain groups (e.g. just the women; or just the men; or just the children), journey around the fire three times; and he watches the fire very closely when someone is circling it for feedback on their mental, physical, and emotional state.

Healings are often done during the portion of the ceremony ruled by the *nagual Keme*. People who need healings are called forward and made to stand with their arms outstretched and their eyes closed while the priest spit / sprays clouds of rum over their bodies. Then when they journey around the fire three times, the priest reads a proper diagnosis and treatment in the flames. In like fashion, petitions for money are usually made during the portion of the ceremony ruled by the *nagual Tzikin*. The participants wave their wallets or purses over the fire and pray to the *nagual Tzikin* to fill them. After the count to thirteen *Tzikin*, the participants are given handfuls of sesame seeds (the *nagual Tzikin*'s favorite treat) to throw into the fire with the wish for money. If the fire should then jump, that is a good omen for the participants' prosperity. Flames tending to the east and north are good but to the west and south not so good. If the participants should throw so much sesame into the fire as to extinguish it (which I saw happen once), the priest in horror will remonstrate with the participants, and explain to them that *nagual Tzikin* is most displeased with their greed and will bring them financial misfortune.

The portion of the ceremony ruled by *nagual Ajmak* is for the expiation of sin. Participants kneel on the ground around the fire and humbly beg forgiveness for their transgressions; and the priest, by observing the behavior of the fire towards each participant, can tell who is holding out; or who has bad karma from ancestors to expiate in this life (which can be ameliorated by performing propitiatory ceremonies on the correct *nagual*). In short, it is by observing the direction in which the flames move that the priest reads how it will go for the person in the particular department of life which that one of the twenty *naguals* symbolizes (and e.g. if the source of the person's problems are due to ancestors).

It should be kept in mind that the information which the priests channel from the fire is usually very down-to-earth (not vague generalities). If participants have asked the priest to divine for specific information (answers to specific questions) before the ceremony began, then at some point during the ceremony the priest usually comes up with the answer. Other predictions the priest seems to pull out of thin air. Once during a ceremony don Abel turned to me and told me that I would soon be involved in a bad land dispute. Sure enough, two weeks later, a land fight started which dragged on for seven years and cost me mucho money and hassles.

On another occasion he told me that I (who up till then had always been very healthy) would soon have a major health problem (and I sensed it meant my legs); and it was a couple of months later that I began to suffer from arthrosis of the hip joint (a degenerative bone disease). At a ceremony done on New Years Day 2009 don Abel told the half-dozen people gathered for it that someone present there would die during the coming year; and don Abel died the following July (in retrospect I believe he knew it meant himself, since he was uncharacteristically gloomy that day). The point is that Mayan ceremonies are quite utilitarian in their purport – not just sterile church services with people mouthing empty formulas – but rather actual connections with the spirit world in which quite practical information and guidance are obtained.

Although all the symbolism of the cardinal directions and the twenty *Chol Qij naguals* provides an intellectual framework to help the priest interpret the omens, what the priest must learn to do is to "read" the message of the fire. To "read" what the fire is saying is very similar to "seeing" what plants are feeling, as explained in the Communicating with Plants chapter. What we are talking about here is known as "operating on sensory thought forms" (using our senses to feel the world) rather than operating on conceptual thought forms (thinking). The motion of the flames – the thought form part – is suggestive; but the information it reveals is more a matter of feeling than of logical deduction.

When lighting a candle to make a prayer or cast a spell, if it is difficult to set up or to light the candle, then it will be difficult for your desire to be realized (there will be obstacles; it will require much work or delay). If the flame wavers or smokes, then this is not a good omen. If the flame is straight and true, then the wish will be granted. If the flame dies or the candle goes out, then the desire will not be realized; or there will be major disappointment in its realization. Wax dripping down the candle can indicate preoccupations; or the demands of other people (that impede).

Flames have auras just as people do; and if you can see auras you can read a lot from them. Cardinal directions can be read from the aura (as well as from the direction the flame leans). If a candle is lit for a person (to ask something for someone) then the aura can be read as if it were that person's aura (for health or emotional information about that person).

If there are dark spots in the flame or in its aura, then there will be troubles (or enemies). If the wish is for health, then the part of the flame (left, right, center, up, down) in which the spots appear indicate trouble areas in the body. If the wish is for money, then e.g. a large flame but a dark spot within it means that the wish will be granted; but the money will soon be lost or will be disappointing. Two or more dark spots in the flame indicate two or more (difficulties, people involved, whatever).

If asking for money for a specific purpose (which is better than asking for money-qua-money), reach into the flame (quickly) with first one hand then the other as if grasping money from it in handfuls of ($10's, $100's, $1000's or whatever denomination of money you are asking for). When you feel a block or your hand gets heavy (after X handfuls), then that's how much money you can expect to get.

If objects on your altar catch on fire, this is a very powerful omen and it behooves you to try to understand the meaning. Once the photograph of my children on my altar burned up. It wasn't until several years later that my spirits explained to me what that was all about: that I should replace that photo (of my kids when they were little, at the ages they were when they were taken away from me) with a photo of them as the adults they are now.

As an example, here's how I interpreted the flames of some of the candles which I lit at a nearby Mayan temple on my last Mayan birthday. Here were my questions and the fire's answers:

1) Should I go forward with a planned surgical operation (a hip replacement), in spite of unfavorable astrological indications (converse progressed Saturn opposition natal moon)? The candle was easy to set up, but I

had dropped it before trying to set it up. The flame fluttered, then burned brightly fluttering. I took this to mean that there will be complications (as the astrology indicates) and may be a slow recovery (fluttering); but that I shouldn't worry about it – everything says "go". (Nb., the operation was successful but it did involve a long and somewhat painful recovery).

2) The nuisance land-dispute lawsuit I am involved in (as plaintiff) – will I win? A strong flame blew towards the south (the Mayan temple of *Chiajxucub*, in which I performed this ritual, has four groups of five *Chol Qij naguals* painted on each of its four walls. The *nagual Tzi*, which rules lawsuits, is one of the five *naguals* painted on the south wall). I took this to be a very favorable omen. While praying I asked to be compensated by the defendants for all the time, energy, and money I had put into this thing; and when I finished this prayer the strong wind blowing the flame towards the right (south) had turned into a gentle breeze; which I took to mean everything will work out okay, not to worry. (Nb. I won the case two years after this omen).

3) Will I be able to sell my land soon, at a good price? The candle was easy to set up and burned with a HUGE flame, also leaning towards the south (where my birth *nagual, Ajmak*, whose day it was, appears on the wall with *Tzi*). I took this to be a definite "yes". (Nb. As of this writing four years later, it hasn't happened yet).

4) Will my best friend and his wife be reunited soon (they lived in different countries for work reasons; and they were about to reunite when she had a stroke and got stuck where she was until medical and financial problems get sorted out)? The tall flame was doubled – burning from the top and side both – which united into one large flame. Then the lower flame fell away down the side of the candle; then both flames went down the side and got together, which turned at last into one big flame. Kind of hard to interpret – obviously there are obstacles in the way, they will reunite for a while but separate again; in the end they will be together and happy. (Nb. They reunited five months later).

5) A friend asks: will she soon become pregnant? The flame wavered feebly in a strong wind towards the south which threatened to blow it out for a long time, until finally the flame burned steadily and normally. I took this to mean that it will be a while yet, or there may be difficulties, in getting pregnant (some sort of karmic issues she has to deal with first); but after a while things will normalize. (Nb: as of this writing four years later she decided to adopt).

6) I did my usual creative visualization about spiritual success and happiness in life; and the flame burned very small, almost timidly. I got the message: "try a little humility for a change." I asked, "About what?" The answer came, "About EVERYTHING!" (I have to point out that my own *nagual*, *Ajmak*, means sin and forgiveness; and this particular Mayan birthday I was directed to do a lot of asking for forgiveness).

These are just some examples of how I interpreted the flames on one occasion. Remember that the thing has to be done by *feeling*, not thinking: it's not the behavior of the flame that is so important, but rather the sense which the flame is communicating. It's similar to the psychic bond you have with a person you are having sex with – things are understood directly.

It is harder to interpret the flames if you have a lot of expectations invested in the matter you are praying or casting a spell for, since if the outcome is super-important to you, the tendency is to engage in wishful thinking – to read the flame the way you want to read it – rather than to feel directly what the flame is saying. On the contrary, you have to let go of your own expectations and be open to whatever is happening. That's all, it's not difficult.

The Purpose of Suffering

Suffering is bearable as long as the sufferer finds some sort of purpose in it. Parents routinely make major sacrifices for the sakes of their children. People go to war – even to certain death – willingly, when they understand that by doing this they are fulfilling a higher purpose – something more important than their own individual pain. If you knew that your suffering was somehow benefiting someone you love; or if you were suffering in place of someone you love; wouldn't you find your suffering worthwhile and easier to bear?

Therefore, the trick of ending your suffering is not by seeking an escape from it (which never seems to work); but rather by finding some kind of purpose in it. Although most people believe that they pity themselves because they are suffering, magicians (and Buddhists) are of the opinion that it actually works the other way around: that it is people's self-pity which is making them suffer. That is, overcoming self-pity vanquishes suffering. But, just as it takes money to make money, so too is it necessary to lose a lot of self-pity first in order to understand why it is advantageous to lose self-pity. Spiritual teachers throughout the ages have agreed that only through suffering can you learn to stop clinging, stop expecting, stop worrying about your own petty little self. Suffering is the only way to learn selflessness.

Real change can only occur when you get completely disgusted with your own self-pity and decide to *really* change. And the only way to arrive at such a decision is by exhaustion: when you've tried this, that, and the other thing; and nothing works. You have to get past the daydream that you are special: that God will miraculously intervene to pull your chestnuts out of the fire for you with no effort on your part. Magicians are convinced – and 12-step programs such as Alcoholics Anonymous concur – that only when a person is completely wiped-out and desperate can any real change occur.

Okay, assuming that you are truly wiped-out and desperate, the next thing to do is to decondition your mindset:

to reprogram the inventory of habitual thoughts which make up your moment-to-moment inner dialogue. Lots of spiritual paths know about and teach this principle: however, they don't usually mention the wiped-out and desperate part, which is an utterly necessary prerequisite. They tell you to "Just think happy thoughts and everything will be wonderful!" However, it is well-nigh impossible, unless you are truly desperate, to stop thinking all your usual thoughts about how unhappy you are. This means not daydreaming or fantasizing about what would make you happy; and also rejecting jealous thoughts about the people who *do* have whatever it is you believe would make you happy. In short, it means to stop thinking about how much you are suffering.

How on earth can you possibly control your thoughts when everything in your life is going horribly? The magician's answer to that is, you can't: it's impossible to do this directly. Rather, you have to trick yourself. This baloney about "just think happy thoughts, and everything will be wonderful!" is true; but it's not true. It's not that simple, because self-pity exerts such a tremendous pull on your feelings. When you have been conditioned all your life to feel self-pity (to feel jealous and insecure and miserable), it's not that easy to just begin feeling happy and accepting and content. To tell someone who is in great pain to "just think happy thoughts!" is like telling someone without legs to just get up and walk. Deconditioning and reconditioning your mindset requires a tremendous amount of time and effort – it's not something you can "just do". It's also why magicians say that there is no point in even considering undertaking the task until you are completely desperate; and even then you have to proceed by self-trickery.

You decondition your mindset by out-and-out lying to yourself, until you actually begin to believe it. For example, a good trick that can help you to find purpose in poverty is to stop comparing yourself to the people who are better off than you are, and instead compare yourself to people who are worse off than you are. Next time you are feeling self-pity about how poor you are, do this: go to a nearby city and stroll around the slum neighborhoods (see – this is what I mean: this isn't that hard to do, but it's the kind of thing which only a truly desperate person actually *would* do).   Stop and talk to the beggars and homeless people you run into. Give them a little money – or better yet, offer to buy them a meal – to begin a conversation.   Listen to their stories.   There's nothing like seeing how much worse off other people are than you to make you realize how lucky you really are, and to make you appreciate all that you do have.

Similarly with illness: it's not that hard to find people who are sicker and in more pain than you are, who perhaps would enjoy companionship or being read to for a few hours a week. It's even more important to do this (compare yourself to people who are worse off than you are rather than to people who are better off than you are) when you are sick, since the tendency with illness is to withdraw into yourself – to focus more and more on your pain – which of course magnifies the pain. Concerning yourself with other people and their pain rather than only your own pain; moving your focus away from how much you are suffering to the suffering of others; is an excellent anodyne.

Okay, once you have started to decondition your mindset – to break your obsessive fixation on thoughts of how unhappy you are by allowing yourself to entertain contrary thoughts – you then have to recondition your mindset. A good place to start reconditioning your thoughts is by asking the question: "What is this suffering teaching me?" In other words, by trying to formulate intellectually the purpose of your suffering. Objectifying your suffering by intellectualizing it is a good way to begin separating yourself from it.

For example, what is the purpose of poverty? In many cases, the lesson to be learned from poverty is to appreciate little things. Rich people never know this feeling, which is why they must compulsively buy and buy and buy in order to fill (temporarily) that emptiness inside themselves, which can only be truly satisfied by a feeling of gratitude and appreciation for what they already have. Only poverty teaches this lesson. Another great lesson which poverty teaches is faith: how to live from day-to-day knowing that somehow or other you'll get by. How can you possibly learn to have faith – trust in the sustaining power of the universe – if you are hedging your bets with so-called "securities"?

What might the purpose of loneliness or rejection be? Perhaps to learn the lesson not to depend upon other people for your happiness; but rather to call up a feeling of self-esteem and self-worth from inside yourself, instead cravenly begging for a pat on the head like a little doggy. How else could you learn this except by rejection and loss? The only way to learn not to cling is to have whatever you are clinging to forcibly stripped from you.

When great tragedies occur, the purpose is often to force you to reorder your priorities: to make you realize what really *is* important in your life. Sometimes it takes a great loss to understand what you actually had, and were taking for granted heretofore. People who have a near brush with death often go through such a reordering of their priorities. They say things like, "Now, I'm just taking it one day at a time." What they are saying is that their eyeball-to-eyeball confrontation with their death has forced them to lighten up, stop clinging to things, stop resenting the past and worrying about the future. They become more selfless. Reordering priorities means to soberly ask the question, "Why did this happen?" instead of moaning and whining "Why did this happen *to me*?" When you can ask yourself that question objectively, then your suffering will start to abate.

One technique which many magicians use to obtain this kind of information – what purpose your suffering is serving you – is to ask for it in dreams. Suppose you want to understand the lesson of your illness. Just before you go to sleep at night, ask with all your heart (determination) that you learn what the purpose of your illness is; what it is that you are seeking to learn from this experience. This technique works best if you can hold the feeling of wanting this information in your mind as you drop off to sleep (it's not possible to hold the actual *thought* in your mind as you drop off to sleep, because thinking is what keeps you awake. Magicians learn how to drop off to sleep with the *desire* – not the actual thought – in their consciousness). You should get the answer either in a dream; or else upon awakening; or perhaps through some offhand remark that someone makes later in the day. It may take more than one night's supplication until the answer comes, so be patient and just keep up the asking every night until the information comes to you.

Another technique which magicians use to understand the purpose which their suffering is serving them is termed *active imagination*. This technique was originated by Carl Jung and is described at length in my book *Thought Forms*. Active imagination enables you to consciously access information that is normally sealed in the repository of your subconscious. In Jung's original formulation, active imagination could be done through any number of arts: music-making, dance, painting, even ceramics. The most straightforward way of doing active imagination is by automatic writing, which can provide more complex and detailed information than dreaming or artistic active imagination does. Automatic writing isn't really difficult: channeling thought forms (which are a part of your subconscious) is done the same way as channeling spirit guides (who are outside of you). Suppose what you want to know about is the reason for your illness. Choose a time when you are relaxed, alert, calm, and will not be interrupted. Lie down or sit, as you prefer, with a pen and notebook in hand (although automatic writing can also be done on a typewriter or word processor). Writing down both your questions and the replies as they come in the form of a dialogue, ask your body to please talk to you. For example, you might start this way: Me: "My body, could you please come and talk to me? I am really trying to be open right now, and I want to hear what you have to say to me. I am trying to understand why I am sick; won't you please come and talk to me about it. Etc. etc."

This is just an example – you should ask your body to talk to you using your own words and sentiments. Keep writing, keep on coaxing, until you begin to feel an answer forming in your mind, and then write it down. The trick to making this work is to not stop writing. Then, simply write down whatever your body tells you about the lesson you are trying to learn from your illness. You can also ask your body for specific information as to diet, exercise, etc. to speed your healing process along.

Similarly, if you want to know the reason for your poverty or loneliness (rather than illness), then call upon your poverty or loneliness to explain it to you. The part of your subconscious which knows the answer will be glad to tell you. The point is that the way to get past suffering isn't by running away from it, but by finding a higher purpose in it; and active imagination is an easy way to do this.

In his book *Man's Search for Meaning*, which describes his experiences as a prisoner at Auschwitz, Dr. Viktor Frankl realized that attending to his patients – who were suffering even more than he was – is what brought him through that nightmare. As Frankl put it: *"Dostoevski said once, 'There is only one thing that I dread: not to be worthy of my sufferings.' These words frequently came to my mind after I became acquainted with those martyrs whose behavior in camp, whose suffering and death, bore witness to the fact that the last inner freedom cannot be lost. It can be said that they were worthy of their sufferings; the way they bore their suffering was a genuine inner achievement. It is this spiritual freedom – which cannot be taken away – that makes life meaningful and purposeful. ... It did not really matter what we expected from life, but rather what life expected from us. We needed to stop asking about the meaning of life, and instead to think of ourselves as those who were being questioned by life – daily and hourly. Our answer must consist, not in talk and meditation, but in right action and in right conduct. ... When a man finds that it is his destiny to suffer, he will have to accept his suffering as his task; his single and unique task. He will have to acknowledge the fact that even in suffering he is unique and alone in the universe. No one can relieve him of his suffering or suffer in his place. His unique opportunity lies in the way in which he bears his burden."*

Appendix: Selections adapted from *Thought Forms*

Merrily, Merrily, Merrily, Merrily

"Someday there will be a great awakening when we know that this is all a great dream. Yet the stupid believe they are awake, busily and brightly assuming they understand things, calling this man ruler, that one herdsman – how dense! Confucius and you are both dreaming! And when I say you are dreaming, I am dreaming, too. Words like these will be labeled the Supreme Swindle. Yet, after ten thousand generations, a great sage may appear who will know their meaning, and it will still be as though he appeared with astonishing speed. ...

"Once Chuang Chou dreamt he was a butterfly, a butterfly flitting and fluttering around, happy with himself and doing as he pleased. He didn't know he was Chuang Chou. Suddenly he woke up and there he was, solid and unmistakable Chuang Chou. But he didn't know if he was Chuang Chou who had dreamt he was a butterfly, or a butterfly dreaming he was Chuang Chou."

– Chuang Tzu

"The self dreams the double. ... Once it has learned to dream the double, the self arrives at this weird crossroad and a moment comes when one realizes that it is the double who dreams the self."

– Carlos Castaneda, *Tales of Power*

"Indeed, perhaps what is now the REM state was the original form of waking consciousness in early brain evolution, when emotionality was more important than reason in the competition for resources. This ancient form of waking consciousness may have come to be actively suppressed in order for higher brain evolution to proceed efficiently. This is essentially a new theory of dreaming."

– Jaak Panksepp, *Affective Neuroscience*

The basic tenet of magic is, that it's all just a dream; that waking consciousness is but a more highly evolved and specialized facet of dream consciousness. Dream consciousness came first evolutionarily, and waking consciousness is an outgrowth of dreaming. Although we tend to believe that there is a vast difference between being awake and dreaming, the fact is that this is indeed merely a belief: a belief which enables us to focus our attention on waking – to isolate it and solidify it – to the exclusion of dreaming.

We make a big deal out of the difference between waking and dreaming, but the distinction between the two states isn't as clear as we usually imagine. When we run past life regressions; or even just listen to music or dance – any time we are so absorbed in any activity that we lose all sense of self perceiving self and are operating on pure "flow" – we are actually closer to being in a dream state than in a waking state. The less we are consciously controlling what is happening, but rather just letting it happen by itself, the closer we are to dreaming. The act of "going to sleep" is just a thought form we use to convince ourselves that we're not dreaming half the time anyway. We use the acts of "going to sleep" and "waking up" to separate out the two modes – to make a distinction where in fact little distinction exists. It's like two people who have been living together for years finally getting married – it's a symbolic thing, there's not much objective difference between the two states. It's as if we made up some sort of distinction like "write with your right hand on Tuesdays, Thursdays, and Saturdays" and "write with your left hand on Mondays, Wednesdays, and Fridays". If we got everyone to do this and make it an automatic habit, then after a few centuries the human race would have invented another distinction in consciousness (indeed, this is in fact what different cultures do). People would find that life on Tuesdays, Thursdays, and Saturdays was very different from life on Mondays, Wednesdays, and Fridays. But it's all an artificial distinction.

Ancient humans were doing what we would consider dreaming as their everyday state of mind. There wasn't as sharp a distinction then between being awake and being asleep. Then people slept in snatches, as infants do, and they alternated hunting off and on with dozing. Most of their hunting was done in a state of mind that we would call sleepwalking (a trance state). They weren't just wandering around aimlessly looking for game to hunt: they could sense what was out there and could project their consciousness forward into their prey telepathically and so anticipate the prey's movements. We moderns can still do this now and then, as for example when on the prowl for sex, or when we sense a business opportunity, especially when we feel lucky; but our hunter forebears relied on this intuitive faculty to eat every day. In other words, ancient hunters were more connected to their world, more psychically attuned, than we moderns are. They were able to pick up information from their environment which eludes us. But on the other hand ancient humans had less sense of a self at center than we do, just as we moderns have less sense of there being a solid, separated "us" there when we are dreaming compared to when we are awake.

Waking consciousness is something which evolves; which can be seen to evolve even between human generations. That's why people "back then" seem so naïve to us – they were dreaming more than we moderns do. We're more awake than our forebears. Consider too how wide-awake First World societies are compared with most Third World societies: First Worlders living in the Third World tend to find the natives to be "irresponsible" and spaced-out, when in fact all they're doing is dreaming more in their everyday waking lives than hup-hup First Worlders do.

The point is that there isn't as hard-and-fast a difference between being awake and dreaming as we are accustomed to believing. It is exactly that belief (that what we do when we are awake is more important than what we do when we are dreaming) which maintains the rigidity of wakefulness – the persuasiveness of the lie that what is happening to us when we are awake is "real" – that is to say, that there is some separated "us" to which things are happening – rather than that the whole shebang is just our projection. That "us" is symbolized by the thought forms of a body, and an outside world in which things happen to that body. When we are dreaming, we have a body also, and a world outside of it. That body and world seem perfectly real while we are dreaming, but when we wake up we realize that it was all just a dream. The interpretation that we have a physical body when we are awake is also merely a belief, exactly like the interpretation that we have a body while we're dreaming is merely a belief. While we are dreaming our dream bodies operate with all five of the usual physical senses. Therefore, we really don't have any objective criteria for deciding, at any given moment, whether we are awake or asleep. In precisely the same fashion, our body when we are awake and the world surrounding it are just a dream. There is no objective difference whatsoever. That's what other people and our society do for us: assure us that we are indeed awake and that what we are experiencing is "real".

Ancient humans were more magical than we are (not as separated). They permitted dream material to freely intrude into their awareness, whereas we moderns have mechanisms in place to immediately repress any such incursion into our reality. When dream stuff intrudes into waking consciousness we get moments of discontinuity. Any sudden start or shock or fright is a rift in our sense of continuity – or better said, a mad grab for our sense of continuity to mask such a rift. We have to say that discontinuity is unreal, and that people who experience discontinuity are crazy, or tired and overworked and in need of rest. We have to get everyone to validate this pretense – to pretend that they're not experiencing discontinuity, in order for society to exist. Society and waking consciousness are just two names for the same thing: in dreams, we are basically alone. In point of fact we're just as alone when we're awake, but we stupidly believe that we are sweating and puffing and bleeding as part of a team. Thus being awake can be defined as the pretense that we're not alone (that we are part of a society).

The reason why the dream state is so mutable is that there is little sense of separatedness in it. It is importance – the sense of urgency, of being driven, of being uptight – which stabilizes attention. We are able to focus our attention when we are awake because of our interminable, self-referent inner chatter every second we are awake. Waking consciousness is a clenching up within oneself – a moment-to-moment flinching from death – embodied in a socially-conditioned striving and intranquility within ourselves that keeps us awake. By contrast, the attention we have in dreams has little importance to it because we don't think so much; but as a result we can't control what we will pay attention to (what will happen next) as well in dreaming as we can when we are awake. What we experience when dreaming is far more immediate, vivid, gripping, and intense than in the ordered waking world. It all happens so fast that we can't separate ourselves from it as we can and do in waking life. We don't get weekends off and two weeks paid vacation in the world of dreams, and there's no TV to watch – no way to make it stop happening or pretend it's not happening. We must either be on the qui vive every instant; or else stand there in a stupor; but we are inevitably so caught up in the dream, so much a part of it, that although we are experiencing our feelings in symbolic form in dreams, there is little sense of separatedness there. Mind exists, but it's not developed.

Mind cannot develop until there is a clearly defined sense of separatedness, which gives mind a pause, a moment's rest or leisure, in which it can reflect on itself. It's that moment's rest or lull which gives birth to a sense of time and linear continuity.

Although waking consciousness originated together with multicellular life on earth, the invention of agriculture was its apotheosis as far as the human species is concerned. As compared with hunting, the invention of agriculture brought order, regularity, sleep 8 hours at night and work 16 hours during the day. Humankind had outgrown dream consciousness; it had found dream consciousness – the consciousness of infants and animals – too unstable, too ephemeral, and therefore too limiting for its free expression. Therefore humans literally constructed, piece by piece, thought form by thought form, over the surface of dream consciousness, the floating edifice of waking mind. Humankind began to think and reason. Separation of quotidian life into 16 hours of wakefulness and 8 hours of dreaming – forcing our bodies to stay awake for such a long stretch of time – is a stern discipline, a way of clenching up, which helps block the intrusion of dream material (magical events) into wakefulness. Ancient humans mixed the two together in their awareness – waking life was as ineffable as dreaming, and everything was a source of wonder and mystery. Native cultures, such as the Mayan people of Guatemala, maintain much of this thought form structure to this day. We North American-European-Asian moderns have learned to tone down our sensory impressions, to separate ourselves from our environment by taking everything around us for granted, by not paying attention to anything except our own incessant mental chatter. This makes our lives utterly boring and meaningless, but nonetheless provides us with our ability to focus our attention, to be methodical, concentrated and deliberate. Our hunter-gatherer ancestors were unable to focus that much attention. They had no need to.

Along with heightened focus comes a decreased sense of connectedness; a greater sense of separatedness. And along with the heightened separatedness necessary to focus attention in the waking world comes a heightened sense of isolation and anguish. In other words, suffering is an intrinsic component of waking consciousness. Without suffering, the constant self-pinching, we could not stay awake.

When we are awake we say "I am suffering!" That "I" is made out suffering (self-pity in the parlance of shamanism). To gainsay Descartes, "I suffer, therefore I am." Just as the waking "I" and the "suffering" arise together, so too do they dissolve together. If "I" ever stop suffering, the disconnected

"I" dissolves too. The main cause of our self-hatred, the chief reason we are all so neurotic and out of kilter with our world, is simply because we've been awake too long. The point is that waking consciousness is not something which is intrinsically different from dreaming, but rather something which evolved and developed out of it; which became more focused and intense and uptight as it evolved. Waking is merely a way of imposing a semblance of order and control (mind – things making some kind of sense instead of being wholly ineffable) on at least a portion of the dream. However this is a falsehood: NOTHING makes any sense – EVERYTHING is ineffable. In other words, waking consciousness – and the society which supports it – is a complete and total fabrication.

Waking mind is like the insouciance of a drunkard staggering across a battlefield where bullets whiz by all around him but who is somehow protected from it all by his blissful indifference. *That* is waking mind. It is so totally a fiction (the sense that we are separated from everything around us) that it can only be maintained by the constant validation of other people (our sense of being part of society). Only by all of us reassuring one another that we are separated individuals – by constantly picking at and annoying each other, just as we constantly pick at and annoy ourselves to stay awake – can we jointly uphold the fragile structure of waking consciousness. Our society assures its continuance by setting its individual members upon each other like ravenous dogs.

When society dissolves because of e.g. war or disaster, everything becomes like a dream, since it's out of control. Waking makes for more control than dreaming, but with a concomitant loss of awareness and joy. Over the next century, as the environment and civilization deteriorate, society will collapse and everything will spin out of control. That is to say, waking consciousness will dissolve back into the dream from which it emerged at the time of the invention of agriculture. The human race isn't going to be able to muddle through this one, as it has always done. Nor will there be any miraculous salvation: no one is going to be raptured up into the clouds to sit next to Jesus; and December 22, 2012 isn't going to be any improvement on December 20th. And certainly the corporations, governments, and materialistic scientists who got us into this mess aren't going to get us out of it. Each individual human being will then be at a crossroads: either lighten up and enter into lucid dreaming as your everyday mode of awareness; or enter into a nightmare.

In the same way that waking consciousness grew out of dreaming, lucid dreaming – that is to say, dreaming in which the dreamer knows that he or she is dreaming – is an outgrowth of waking consciousness. Lucid dreaming is humankind's next step in the evolution of consciousness – New, Improved, Lemon-Scented Consciousness. It's also our only hope for survival as a species.

Lucid dreaming allows us to take a pause for reflection on the dream plane: to make it stop happening for a moment to critically evaluate and redirect the experience, instead of being wholly caught up in it, forced to be constantly shifting and adjusting ourselves to it, as our hunter forebears had to do. Hunters had to more or less go with the flow, and they were better or worse hunters as they were able to be flexible and quick to see and grasp opportunities and avoid pitfalls as they arose. They were nimble, but not very capable of planning, organizing, or thinking things through. If there was an easier way to do something, they probably wouldn't have been able to figure it out (not enough separatedness).

What happens in lucid dreaming is that we preserve the thought forms of waking consciousness, but without the importance. That is to say, lucid dreaming is waking consciousness without the driving urgency, the constant uptightness, the sense of a separated, suffering succotash of a self. We still have a self, symbolized by a body thought form, while we are lucidly dreaming; but that body is a great deal lighter and less separated than our waking body. It can fly, for one thing.

The point is, as all lucid dreamers soon realize, that the thought forms of waking consciousness can be activated in the dream state once they have been cut loose from their importance. Lucid dreaming is what waking consciousness could be (and will be) like when we get rid of our importance. To do lucid dreaming consistently we will have to come to a general conviction in our daily lives that nothing is all that important. It is the purpose of the practice of magic to make everyday life more like dreaming – to release the fixation on a separated, suffering self. This is accomplished by cultivating the practice of lucid dreaming while we are asleep, and by going to trees or nature spirits every day while we are awake. The doorway out of wakefulness into lucid dreaming is what magicians term sensory thought forms, and what cognitive philosophers term *qualia*: that is to say, shifting attention from thinking to feeling the world around us. This entails quieting down our minds and listening to sounds, feeling the breeze on our skin, seeing the plants and the clouds. It's what mystics refer to as "suchness" or "thusness"; but really all it involves is just shutting up the constant stream of mental chatter long enough to see – hear – feel what's going on in the now moment – i.e., to do what we do when we're dreaming while we're awake. The "Following Feelings" chapter described how to do this. The practice of recapitulation, described in my book *The Great Wheel*, is also extremely invaluable in releasing the obsessive fixation of waking consciousness; releasing our obsessive grip on everyday life and the people around us.

The goal for us as individuals is to merge dreaming and waking – to be as light and unencumbered while awake as we are while dreaming; and to be as rational and clear-thinking while dreaming as we are when we are awake. The goal for us humans as a species is to make lucid dreaming our everyday awareness, in the same way that our hunter-gatherer ancestors made waking consciousness their everyday awareness at the time that agriculture was invented. I.e., to become magicians.

The purpose of Buddhism – at least insofar as I understand it – is to get a few exceptional people fully enlightened. The purpose of the practice of magic is to get the mass of people somewhat enlightened – i.e. enlightened enough to save the human race and the earth. No major upheaval in present society would necessarily be required to make this shift, unless humankind stupidly proves to be incapable of responding short of a total crisis. There are probable realities which go either way, which we as individuals can choose or decline to participate in, by believing what we choose to believe. All that's required to save humanity is for most people (not necessarily all) to lighten up just a little bit. We don't need everyone to don sackcloth and ashes and take to caves and become enlightened; nor do we need everyone to fall in line and believe as we do. All we need is for most people to become just a tad less greedy, selfish, suspicious, intolerant, closed-hearted and shameless. Just for most people to lighten up a teensy bit is all that's required for the human race to enter into lucid dreaming together.

In the state of lucid dreaming everyone instantly knows the truth, so pretense is impossible. By contrast, most of what transpires in waking consciousness is a pack of lies: people are talking about one thing, but what is really going on under the surface is something altogether different. It isn't like that in lucid dreaming – what we see is what we get. There's no room for phoniness because those importance coverings don't exist in lucid dreaming – that agreement is more important than truth.

Yes, Virginia, Truth does indeed exist. All that's necessary to find it is to cut through all the yada-yada nonsense of our decadent, degenerate society and listen to what our hearts are telling us. We magicians do this by going to trees and nature spirits for validation rather than to our fellow humans.

To enter into lucid dreaming from a position which starts from being awake is the same thing as astral projection. Talented dreamers have a facility for astral projection, and this can be the quickest way for them to go. But it would take most people too long to learn astral projection; it's easier for them to come at it through lucid dreaming. This is a better path for people who think too much, since it minimizes thinking. We have to start from being asleep, and then beckon our separatedness thought form to come to us without its covering of importance. If the covering of importance comes too, then we wake up. That's why so many of us find it difficult to maintain ourselves in a state of lucid dreaming without waking up: one must be calm in a lucid dream, otherwise one tends to beckon importance.

Lucid dreaming is not something essentially different from waking consciousness, only we get to it from a position of being asleep. When we start out from a position of being awake, we call it "everyday life". What do you suppose the horseless carriage is? Or the radio, TV, airplane, space rocket, computer? They are all wild, crazy dreams. A hundred years ago that's exactly what we would have considered them. And that's all they are – dreams. Humankind just incorporated that dream material into waking consciousness. That's the sort of thing waking consciousness is good for: to originate dream material of that sort. That kind of business requires slow, patient development over generations; and the dream plane is too unstable and mutable to do that kind of stuff on. The dream plane is too here and now. Since dream consciousness is more timeless than waking consciousness, it doesn't allow for the detachment that a sense of past (history) and future (planning) can give. We need a greater sense of separatedness to be able to do things that slowly. That's why it is so difficult to do things like dial a phone number or read a sentence in a normal dream – these activities require a greater degree of separatedness than normal dreaming affords, to be able to bring that kind of minute detail into focus.

That's the genius of waking consciousness: we lose scope and agility, but in return we get focus and a methodical way of getting at things. Waking consciousness is much more clearly focused and delimited than dreaming, even if we all become extremely myopic and uptight in the process.

The practice of magic is about turning our everyday waking lives into lucid dreaming, cultivating a somewhat "altered state of mind" as our everyday mindset. As we do this much of our sense of separatedness dissolves and we feel more inner peace and oneness with our world. Spirits start talking to us, as they did to our hunter-gatherer ancestors. Our everyday life becomes more like dreaming – i.e., more magical. This is the road that each of us must travel as individuals; and which the human race as a whole will have to follow if it is to survive and prosper. It is the road of entering into a state of lucid dreaming from a position which starts from being awake (instead of asleep, as usual). This means understanding that waking consciousness *is* lucid dreaming; and the only reason we can't see that is because we must keep up the pretense that what we're doing is "real" and important. Therefore we can't see that it's all just a dream.

At this writing there don't seem to be too many lucid dreamers out there; but there are lots of people merrily, merrily, merrily, merrily dancing a jig on their descent into the coming nightmare. It's time now for everyone to wake up.

The Reification of Time

"At one time I waded through the river and at one time crossed the mountain. You may think that that mountain and that river are things of the past, that I have left them behind and am now living in this palatial building – they are as separate from me as heaven is from earth.

"However, the truth has another side. When I climbed the mountain and crossed the river, I was time. .... I have always been; time cannot leave me. When time is not regarded as a phenomenon which ebbs and flows, the time I climbed the mountain is the present moment of being-time. When time is not thought of as coming and going, this moment is absolute time for me. ...

"Do not regard time as merely flying away; do not think that flying away is its sole function. For time to fly away there would have to be a separation between it and things. Because you imagine that time only passes, you do not learn the truth of being-time. In a word, every being in the entire world is a separate time in one continuum. And since being is time, I am my being-time. Time has the quality of passing, so to speak, from today to tomorrow, from today to yesterday, from yesterday to today, from today to today, from tomorrow to tomorrow. Because this passing is a characteristic of time, present time and past time do not overlap or impinge upon one another."

– Dogen-zenji

"(The Daimon, or Oversoul) does not perceive, as does the human mind of man, object following object in a narrow stream, but all at once, & because it does not perceive objects as separated in time & space, but arranged alone as it were in the order of their kinship with itself, those most akin the nearest & not as they are in time & space."

– William Butler Yeats

"The shamans of ancient Mexico never regarded time and space as obscure abstracts the way we do. For them, both time and space, although incomprehensible in their formulations, were an integral part of man.

"Those shamans had another cognitive unit called the wheel of time. The way they explained the wheel of time was to say that time was like a tunnel of infinite length and width, a tunnel with reflective furrows. Every furrow was infinite, and there were infinite numbers of them. Living creatures were compulsorily made, by the force of life, to gaze into one furrow. To gaze into one furrow alone meant to be trapped by it, to live that furrow.

"A warrior's final aim is to focus, through an act of profound discipline, his unwavering attention on the wheel of time in order to make it turn. Warriors who have succeeded in turning the wheel of time can gaze into any furrow and draw from it whatever they desire. To be free from the spellbinding force of gazing into only one of those furrows means that warriors can look in either direction: as time retreats or as it advances on them."

– Carlos Castaneda

Contrary to popular belief, space and time have no objective existence. Therefore, to base our science and philosophy – not to mention our everyday lives – upon the assumption of reified space and time is about as absurd as basing them on the existence of Santa Claus and the Easter Bunny. Indeed, Santa Claus and the Easter Bunny are considerably more real in the cosmic scheme of things than what we call "space" and "time".

Space and time are merely tools – techniques for organizing cognition – which evolved as sentient beings evolved. Just as the sense of vision is a cognitive tool which evolved as animals evolved; and visual acuity is more pronounced in predatory animals such as eagles than it is in e.g. blind cave fish; so too are the sense of space and time cognitive tools which are sharper (more highly evolved) for humans than for "lower" animals. The belief that they are centered in space and time enables beings to focus attention upon one thing at a time instead of everything at once; and also gives rise to the sense that there is a separated being which is focusing this attention.

What time really is, is not how we perceive it to be in our normal, everyday consciousness; any more than what love really is, is not how we perceive it to be when we are infatuated. Although human perception and cognition make sense to humans, the universe itself doesn't make sense in the way that humans believe. There is no space or time out there.

Where materialistic science sees time as linear, magical science sees time as rhythmic. Materialistic science measures points and intervals along a well-ordered continuum, whereas magical science measures cycles upon cycles. This is what astrology is all about: the moment of birth can be viewed as a point along a linear continuum, as it is in materialistic science; or, conversely, it can be viewed as a stage in the unfoldment of potentialities on various levels – i.e. as the intersection of many different interpenetrating cycles, as it is in astrology.

It is more accurate to describe time as an emanation of birth – death – rebirth. The so-called real number system has no model in nature: the universe is not continuous, but rather explodes into being and dissolves into nothingness with every passing instant of "time". What we take to be linear time is but a fragmentary way of apprehending and dealing with this phenomenon, which has evolved in tandem with human consciousness.

While animals are vaguely aware of the passage of time – i.e. while animals also organize their cognition temporally – animal consciousness is far less focused than human consciousness. Animals have far less sense of being separated individuals than humans have – they have less awareness of a separated self, are less "there" than humans feel themselves to be; and as a result their experience of time is less "there" as well.

We humans – especially we modern humans, are in a big hurry. Being in a big hurry is how we define ourselves. "We" are something that is in a big hurry; being in a big hurry is what "we" are made out of. Linear time is a completely human invention, like golf or the latest Paris fashions – a set of rules which have no reference to anything outside of human experience. Linear time is predicated on linear thinking. When linear thinking stops – when the constant internal dialogue which most people engage in from the minute they awaken to the minute they go to sleep ceases – then so too does linear time.

The argument in favor of linear time really boils down to the old post hoc ergo propter hoc fallacy – that things make sense because they make sense; that there's a reason why this and not that; that everyday life, our experience of waking reality, is not just a dream – a mere flood of random hypnagogic hallucinations to which we quite arbitrarily (and unskillfully) attribute sequence and causality: "First this happened, then that happened, then the other thing happened; and that's who I am. That's how I define my self as an individual – my sense of being centered in a body, in a world, in a reality!"

In hypnagogic hallucination – the flood of images which pass through our minds as we are dropping off to sleep – we can view the process by which we create our own dream reality; our waking reality is created analogously. In waking life, as in hypnagogic hallucination, there is no reason why this image or situation is chosen and not that one. Reasons why things are have to be cobbled together in retrospect, to provide a post hoc justification for why things are the way they are. Although causes do give rise to effects, and these effects are even predictable at times, there is in truth no reason why this and not that. In other probable realities it came out that and not this.

While brain research being carried out in neuroscience will undoubtedly lead to many useful discoveries, it has nothing to do with the study of consciousness. The so-called physical brain, like the physical body it inhabits, is merely a projection of the mind, exactly in the same fashion that the dreaming body is a projection of the mind. The only difference is that the waking body and brain are persistent enough for us to dissect. If we could make dreaming hold still long enough to examine minutely we would find that our dream bodies and brain were made out of molecules and cells and neurons and whatnot too. Or whatever. The only reason why stuff is made out of molecules and cells instead of fire, earth, air, and water is because that's the way science went in this particular probable reality. But none of this actually exists, it's all just a dream – an arbitrary hypnagogic hallucination.

In the magical model moment-to-moment decisions are not made by mind, much less by a physical brain; they are merely reflected in mind. Mind conjures up reasons after the fact to justify the decisions that have already been made on a level of feeling (dreamless sleep). In the magical view decisions are made "first", and then circumstances arise "later" which reflect those decisions; i.e. everyone creates their own reality.

That is to say, mind – and the so-called physical brain – are like the scoreboard at an athletic contest. The scoreboard reflects what is happening on the field, but it doesn't create it. Similarly, mind and the brain reflect decisions that are being made on a feeling level, but they certainly don't create anything. They don't even apprehend anything. They just keep count, keep score, keep tabs on what is really going on. A body – whether in dreaming or waking – is merely a counter: first this happens to it, then that happens to it, then the other happens to it, then it dies.

The actual situation is one of complete randomness – of all likely outcomes occurring simultaneously in different probable realities. And in each probable reality mind clicks out a thought form to justify / explain why this or that particular reality occurred. E.g. there is no "competition for scarce resources" going on; this is just the presenting problem, the superficial appearance of an energy dynamic in which sentient beings appear to be in turmoil, preying upon and devouring one another's energy. This is what W.B. Yeats' termed Deception – the appearance that the acts of creation and destruction are not exactly identical, flip sides of the same coin, like the snake devouring its own tail. Elephants don't have long proboscises because this confers an evolutionary advantage. Rather, they just have them, period. Any evolutionary advantage this bestows is a post hoc, materialistic interpretation: things are the way they are because that's how they are, and this explains why they are that way

Anyone who discerns any purpose in the outworkings of the universe – whether this purpose is conceived of as the will of God, or survival of the fittest and most prolific reproducers, or the selfishness of genes – is looking at things backwards. Both Christianity and rationalistic materialism (academic pseudo-science) are projecting images which aren't there. Like the cabalistic Gematria which finds hidden connections in every biblical name and phrase, or like a paranoid who detects sinister plots against him in every chance occurrence, Christianity and materialism project meaning and purpose onto complete chaos. There is no purpose to anything except as in retrospect it can be argued that things are the way they are because that is how they were meant to be. But this is an illusion, the post hoc ergo propter hoc fallacy, which in turn is predicated on the fallacy of linear time.

This is not to say that there is no causality in the universe: effects do not arise without a cause. However that causality is not embedded in linear time, and indeed it is too complex to analyze rationally (though here and there its results can be anticipated or predicted by intuition / feeling, as we do in astrology). What most of us take to be causality is merely an illusion – mistaking how humans in our society make agreements amongst themselves for laws of the universe; as if golf or the latest Paris fashions were somehow universal principles with application outside of human society. What we take to be causality is merely post hoc sophistry: "See, I told you so!" But it doesn't prove anything whatsoever.

For example, we mistakenly believe that first things happen to us, and then we react to them. E.g., first we get laid off from our job, and then we feel depressed and helpless. However from the magical point of view, the decision to feel depressed and helpless is primary – is made "first" (on the level of dreamless sleep). The "getting laid off" thought form is conjured up "later" (on the level of waking consciousness) to justify feelings of importance – that it's important to feel depressed and helpless. In astrology we can often see bad times coming up in the future, in the progressions or transits, although it's not always possible to predict the exact thought form situation which the bad times will take. The point is that either causality has nothing to do with linear time; or else astrology is a false doctrine. Q.E.D.

If we're going to understand this point of view we have to get over our prejudice, which is all it is, about time being linear. The fact is that time is not linear. Here's a way of looking at it: survivors of near-death experiences often report having seen every single event that ever happened to them during their lives flash by them in no time at all. Sometimes they report seeing everything that ever happened to them zip by, but still being able to see each scene discretely, in a few seconds' time. Others report seeing each individual event of their entire lives in one, complete take. In any case, it would seem that we experience the thought forms of our lives twice: once in linear fashion over a lifetime, and then in a timeless fashion (everything at once) at the moment of death.

This idea that time can be non-linear is easiest to see in dreams. Dream time is sequential, but not linear in the same sense in which waking time is linear. Dream time doesn't have the same cause-and-effect inexorability that waking time has. This is because there is less focus in dreams, so everything is more here-and-now. Unlike waking consciousness, in dreaming we are rarely influenced by past or future events. We don't define ourselves in terms of personal history and future so much as we do when we're awake. Things happen too fast and too intensely in dreams to dwell upon: everything is just too vivid and too now.

When we are awake and confronted by a life-threatening situation, e.g. while we are having an automobile accident or during a big earthquake, time slows way down. We can see everything that is happening with great clarity, in great detail, as if it were unfolding in slow-motion. This slow-motion perception of time is closer to the truth. Slow-motion perception is more like how infants and ancient humans perceived time. It is more like dream-time perception and less like our modern, everyday, gloss-over-things-quickly-and-superficially-in-a-big-hurry perception of time. Buddhists aver that experienced meditators are capable of slowing time down enough to be able to discern and distinguish individual thought forms (sankhara), desires (vedana), and moods (sanna) at the instant they arise. However, it is impossible to act in the normal way in this slow-motion perception of time because we can't think. If we are going to act or react in this frame of mind, we can only do so on intent, on our gut-level instinct, not on thought. Therefore the slow-motion perception is not as useful in performing all the humdrum tasks of modern, everyday life as is normal time perception; but it is the more useful form of perception in the practice of magic (as it was in hunting), where decisions have to be made faster than normal thinking allows.

When time slows down enough we lose our sense of separated selfhood altogether and move into altered states of consciousness. Indeed, we can define "altered state" as the feeling of timelessness. This can happen due to shock, psychedelic drugs, or even spirits. Some spirits have the power to temporarily erase our importance (self-pity) so that we experience a state of selfless grace. Enlightenment is such a state – people who are enlightened can move into and out of timelessness and selflessness at will, by focusing their attention one way or the other. But even enlightened people don't exist in a state of nirvana all day long. They have normal lives to lead too, and altered states are not particularly functional in everyday society. That's why our modern time sense evolved: it is more functional for agriculturalists than the NOW time sense of hunting-gathering.

Altered states can be inspiring, can give us a glimpse of the goal we are shooting for, but they are always temporary. Normal, everyday life is the battleground, the place where the real work has to be done, the place where it all begins and ends. The goal of magical training is to bring an awareness of timelessness and selflessness (which are the same thing) into the routines of our everyday lives. We do this by detaching from the hurried me-me-me with its endless fluster of self-pitying moods from the past and concerns for the future.

Linear time is the matrix of our separated, lower self. Self and time arise together and fall together (dissolve into selflessness and timelessness). Our hunter-gatherer ancestors, like infants, didn't have anywhere near as much sense of a separated self as we moderns do. They were not as individuated as we are today. They paid more attention to their feelings, their intuition, than to their thinking. Ancient humans lived in a more timeless frame of mind, a sense of belonging to the universe. Their mental processing wasn't a matter of constant thinking, but rather of direct knowing what their ancestors, spirits, and the earth were telling them. They felt themselves to be part of an ongoing, natural process in the same way that we feel ourselves to be part of our society. Because they were not as separated as we are today, they felt less *Angst* than we do, because they had no future to worry about.

If the future didn't exist, would we care about it? If we stop thinking so much about the past and future, then the past and future lose much of their meaning. They are just not as important, so they are not as "there", just as they aren't as "there" for infants or ancient humans as they are for us. Infant and ancient human consciousness isn't a matter of the constant dissatisfaction and relentless striving which enables modern humans to focus enough attention to think.

When humans were still hunters, they did not draw as sharp a distinction between being awake and being asleep as we do today, since they slept in snatches when they felt like it instead of in long stretches during the night. Similarly, they didn't draw as sharp a distinction between past and future as we do now because they didn't need to – they were more centered in the now moment, hence they experienced their past and future in a more immediate fashion than we do today. They didn't define themselves as much in terms of personal history (moods) and future aspirations (concerns).

We say, "I am no longer who I was back then" – separating who we are now from who we were at an earlier age. We say, "Someday I will be or do such-and-such" – separating who we are now from who we fantasize we will become. But our hunter-gatherer ancestors didn't have that much of a sense of separatedness – things that happened to them a long time ago, or that would happen to them some future day (what we would call prescience or sense of destiny), were more a part of who they conceived themselves to be now than they are for us. They were in closer touch with their intent – the feeling of their past and future; they didn't have as many thought forms interposing a linear order upon their consciousness, imposing some ponderous past and inexorable future upon their present.

It's precisely us moderns' caring and worrying about the future that conjures up its existence. We care about the future, it's important to us, because we believe there's glory for us somewhere in our future – that we're going to win the lottery, or find true love, or become famous, or go to heaven, or some other such fantasy. What impels each of us individuals forward through time is the mirage of instant relief from our sufferings and release from our bondage – that miraculous change of luck that we imagine is just over the next hill.

The other side of that coin is our past, the things that we are ashamed of and would never reveal to anyone (and are trying to forget about ourselves).

The carrot and stick of striving towards a glorified future and slinking away from a shameful past is what creates the illusion that there is such a thing as a future and a past. When striving ends, so too does linear time. Without these constant, driving concerns we enter into a state of timelessness. This is what we experience in altered states of awareness. In altered states we just don't give a damn about the past or future – we're too centered and joyous and at one with things in the present.

Feeling is spatial; that is, what we call space is merely our sense of having feelings and what we call time is our sense of having thoughts – hence everyone's need for their own personal space or right to their own feelings, and their own time to make up their minds. Physical, three-dimensional space is a symbol for feelings, just as time is a symbol for thoughts; hence space still exists in the dream state, but time doesn't – at least not in the same sense in which it exists in the waking state. Our sense of personal continuity in the dream state is not based upon a linear, sequential, unfolding of events, as it is in waking. Things jump around too much in dreams for us to be able to operate on the assumption of personal continuity such as we make in our everyday lives in waking consciousness. Rather, our sense of selfhood in dreaming is based upon an awareness of self as experiencer (i.e., of death).

The point is that what we call time is a falsehood. To us moderns space and time are real, and feelings and thoughts are symbols for space and time; but in fact, exactly the reverse is true. Linear time is an illusion similar to the illusion of motion produced by the series of still pictures which make up a movie. Babies (and even young children, who sometimes talk about memories from other lifetimes) are not as centered in a one-track existence as adults are. Babies and young children are consciously impinged upon by influences (feelings) from other lives and probable realities which most adults have learned to ignore. The same socialization process which props up a baby's sense of being a unitary, abiding, separated individual also imprisons that individual in a furrow of inexorable linear temporality.

In other words, the illusion that time is linear – that there is a sensible progression from one moment to the next – is merely an agreement that human beings make. Just as during courtship people focus entirely on the positive aspects of their relationship and ignore the negative ones; and later when the marriage falls apart all they focus on are the negatives and ignore the positives; in the same way people focus all their moment-to-moment attention on that which seems to be familiar and persistent. But the truth is that each passing moment is an entirely new ballgame with completely different rules: nothing persists, and everything is ineffable. Familiarity is a lie people tell themselves and each other to keep from losing their marbles: "Oh no, I'm not completely disoriented here, everything's just fine and dandy!" It's this lie that makes society (waking consciousness) possible.

Crazy people, retarded people, and master magicians can't buy into this lie (that the universe isn't as chaotic, ineffable and out-of-control as dreaming). They can't (nor do they necessarily want to) assemble waking consciousness as effectively as "normal" people do. Nor do they experience time in the same fashion.

Time isn't a line. It's more like a plane, an infinite-ring circus, an eternal NOW moment, in which everything that has ever happened and ever will happen, in all lifetimes and realities, is happening all at once. But each individual thought form involved thinks that it is a real, separated being with individual self-existence and a personal history and future. Each of the infinite thought forms which make up "us" – all of the things we have ever experienced or ever will experience; all of the monads of every instant of awareness in all our probable realities from this life and all our past and future lives – thinks that it is the real "us", centered in a universe in which things make sense. Each individual thought form (since they are indeed discrete) thinks it's the top dog (most important). And from any given thought form we can move to an infinite number of possible futures or remember an infinite number of possible pasts. And once that decision is made – the decision to move from the standpoint of any given thought form now moment to any other given thought form future moment or remembered past moment – mind will stamp upon that decision the notation: MAKES SENSE! (is "real"). That's the only reason why things make sense (seem real) to us: because we are constantly telling ourselves the lie that things make sense. We tell ourselves the same lie when we are dreaming (that what we are experiencing makes sense, is "real").

Admittedly, some probable futures or pasts are more likely than others; it's more likely that your next thought form will be moving a bit further along reading this sentence rather than suddenly appearing on a Caribbean beach sipping a piña colada. That's the sort of thing that happens in dream consciousness – the jump from thought form to thought form tends to be a lot more haphazard than in waking consciousness. But it's nonetheless a random process, shaped by tendencies from human and individual memory, whose only claim to fame is that it makes sense – there's no doubt about it!

Mind is what makes sense out of this selection. This is easier to see in dream consciousness where even the most bizarre and improbable (from the point of view of wakefulness) thought forms can pop up and yet make perfect sense at the time we are dreaming them. Similarly, our waking consciousness (experience of everyday life) also only makes sense because we have decided to let it make sense. That assumption is what traps us in our furrows.

To lose our sense of linear time implies living moment-to-moment with all of our memories – at least the feeling of them if not the actual thought forms. Only by recapitulating all of our memories, as explained in my book *The Great Wheel*, are we in possession of all the memories (feelings) of all our past and probable lives, as well as this one. At that point we're not really centered in any given one of them anymore. The waking state is controllable only as long as it seems familiar and important – i.e., centered in a past and future. The trick, then, is to be quite comfortable with everything out of control, as it were. To just stop floundering around and float with the current. When we stop trying to control things, then we are dreaming. The more out of control we let our daily lives be, the more we are actually dreaming rather than being awake, and the closer we are to our intent – to being able to act on our true feelings rather than our social conditioning. This is what the practice of magic is all about.

Death is Watching

When we listen to sounds, we can distinguish between two phenomena: "sounds" and "listener listening to sounds":

"Sounds" is when we are hearing all sounds indiscriminately, like a tape recorder does; when all sounds are impacting on our awareness with equal vividness.

"Listener listening to sounds" is when we are focusing on one specific sound, and the other sounds are in the background of our awareness. That "listener listening to sounds"– that focus, or sense of there being a detached perceiver there who is perceiving – is what magicians call lower self. At least, that is what dies when the person's body dies. When there is no longer a sense of a separated perceiver perceiving, when everything is impacting upon our awareness with equal vividness, what is left is a feeling of oneness, a background of peacefulness, which is what magicians call higher self, or death. Death is in the background all the time. Death is the canvas upon which our lives are painted.

When we feel that we are watching ourselves – that there is some part of us that is watching our every move – that part is our death. It is constantly looking over our shoulder; it's the sense we have that something out there is watching us (the Spirit is watching us too, not to mention lots of other beings, both angelic and demonic; but our root self-consciousness, the sense that we feel within ourselves that something is watching us, is our death).

Observe that this is not the false watcher thought form, which we use to watch ourselves with glory, and exalt in how marvelous we are. That watcher is a phony copy of the true watcher – death – which is utterly cold and dispassionate. The false watcher – our self-consciousness, or need to keep referring everything back to ourselves – is a thought form which takes anything that is going on and glamorizes it, and imagines other people applauding us for it. We learn the false watcher thought form from our society: the false watcher thought form is in fact society's way of papering over death.

We do have a true watcher watching us, and that watcher is our death. The false watcher is society's way of eradicating death from people's awareness, to make people act as if they weren't going to die, to make people forget about death as much as possible. Only by making people forget about death can they be led into believing that there could be anything more important than the fact that they could die in the next instant. And part of banishing awareness of death is substituting a glory thought form of watching ("watching oneself in glory; watching oneself with approval / approbation") for the true watcher thought form, which is death.

Another way of saying this is: the sense we have that we are perceiving; that there is some detached perceiver there perceiving; that there is some "us" there to which things are happening; is our death. Without that sense of a detached perceiver there, we wouldn't be able to focus on anything. Everything that we see, hear, touch, etc. at every moment – not to mention bleed-throughs from other lifetimes and probable realities – would bombard our senses with equal impact. We would be overwhelmed with information; indeed, we would have no sense that "we" exist at all (just as an infant doesn't) – we would be pure perception. This is a common experience when one is tripping on psychedelic drugs: for example, when we take a shower while tripping, we can feel (are aware of) every individual drop of water as it hits our skin as a discrete event. On the other hand we can't balance a checkbook while tripping because we can't focus that much attention – there's too much going on to be able to focus. To use mind – to be able to focus on one thing at a time by separating it out from its background – is to create a perceiver which is perceiving; and that's what we call death.

When we say that death is watching, what we're saying is that the act of watching is what we mean by death. Anything that watches will die. This is because watching – separatedness – is a lie which eventually must run out. Separatedness is a lie which all sentient beings tell themselves. That lie is what embeds them in linear time. If a vortex in a river were to suddenly start saying to itself something like "I'm a vortex! I'm a vortex! I'm a unique, individual, separated vortex!" then that vortex would be lying to itself – it's not a unique, individual, separated anything. But by telling itself that lie, it embeds itself in a linear temporality in which it watches this, and then it watches that, and then it watches the other thing; until the vortex runs out of energy and dissolves back into the river and stops lying to itself about having been separated in the first place – i.e., it dies. But it was "dead" all along. Watching = separatedness = death; they are just different ways of talking about the same phenomenon.

Our sense of personal continuity in the dream state is not based upon a linear, sequential, unfolding of events, as it is in the waking state, but rather is based upon an awareness of self as experiencer (i.e., one's death). That vibrant, alive quality that dreams have is actually awareness of death. In dreams we are aware of death every second, willy-nilly, because there's nothing solid in dreams to cling to: there's no way of toning down the intensity of what we are experiencing by focusing our attention elsewhere (on our thoughts). We're face-to-face with death every second in dreams. That's why we feel more alive in dreams than we do in wakefulness – because we are seeing with the eyes of death; we are one with death when we are dreaming, which is why we can't die in dreams – we're already dead. In wakefulness we make a separation between ourselves and our deaths – an absurd pretense, but a useful one for certain purposes (such as being able to focus attention enough to e.g. balance a checkbook) – and that's why wakefulness is duller, less vivid, less joyous than dreaming.

Here's the answer to the mystery: what we consider to be "ourselves" is just a given thought form at a given moment. Our lifetimes are like a collection of scenes or tableaux strung together by mind into a lattice of threaded beads. All of the beads (or life events) which directly connect to a given bead are probable realities. From that bead, mind can take any number of directions to another bead. The black threads connecting the beads are death – we literally die from moment-to-moment. We always have to pass through death to move to the next bead (the next scene; the next moment); and if we take a turn which leads to a long run of black thread till the next bead, that's "real" death and the next bead is birth in another lifetime.

Another way of saying this is, we have ourselves separated into a bunch of little pieces, each of which feels isolated and disconnected from (more important than) the rest. However, within each little piece we have tremendous focus and stick-to-itiveness ("fear of death") – a willingness to keep up the struggle to stay awake and separated no matter how much of a bummer it is.

The "you" who is reading this sentence is actually a very different being than the "you" who read the previous sentence, and this is not meant in a trivial sense (that a few cells have split in the interim) – it is meant in the deepest sense possible. The belief that you are the same person from moment to moment is an illusion, a lie. To maintain this illusion you must snatch yourself back from death every instant, be on the qui vive every second. It is precisely this clenching up against death which creates and sustains waking consciousness (gives us the focus and control we lack in dreaming, e.g. the ability to balance a checkbook). This is why we are so uptight when awake compared to how open and vulnerable we are in dreaming. To maintain waking consciousness requires incredible fortitude and self-discipline (not to mention completely lying to ourselves every second that we are awake).

In actual fact, we are nothing more than our death. Our death is the complete written record of our life. It is all contained in our death. Our death can be likened to a microdot which contains our entire life in one little point. We are like the little point which moves on an Etch-a-Sketch board or computer drawing program, blazing out a path through life (making a squiggle on a previously blank screen) and leaving a trail behind it. The entirety of our being is like that blank screen, and the squiggly path is this particular lifetime. It has a beginning and an end, and is delimited. That delimitation is death.

In other words, just as our sense of space is our sense of having feelings (familiarity); and our sense of time is our sense of having thoughts (importance – our ability to focus our attention); so too is our death our sense that there is some contained entity which is having those feelings and thoughts. Death is our sense of containment, of boundedness, of singularity, of discreteness. It is a species of glue which binds random feelings and thought forms together into an integrated, cohesive whole.

Death projects a body thought form to symbolize this sense of discreteness, solidity, stability, boundedness – just as we project a body thought form when we are dreaming, to symbolize "us". What we consider our unity – our individuality, our continuity, our "us-ness" – is actually our death. When we cling to our sanity, our sense of being centered in a stable environment where things are more or less predictable, what we are clinging to is our death. Wakefulness could not exist without it.

Observe that in reality there is no such distinction as importance – but if we were to say that one is more important than the other, certainly our death is more important than (primary to) our life. Our life is just a symbolic reflection of our death; it's not the main issue at all. To think that our life is more important than our death is not only gross stupidity, but plays right into death's hands.

Death is neither malevolent or benevolent – it just is, like the force of gravity. Gravity can both hurt us and help us, depending upon how we use it (or let ourselves be used by it). So too with death. Death actually calls all the shots and we have to dance to its tune, really; but we can do that either elegantly or spasmodically. Master magicians waltz with their death; caress it fondly; and then seduce it.

Importance – that is to say, focus: our ability to focus attention – is the means by which we consolidate death, or grab onto it (though what we believe we're doing is pushing it away). Importance is the illusion that we are controlling our death, when actually the reverse is the case. It's like hanging on for dear life to a runaway stallion and all the while trying to pretend that everything's just fine and dandy. The runaway stallion we cling to is death, and the pretense that we are in any way, shape, or form in charge of the situation is importance. It's what keeps us from enjoying the scenery as we gallop along.

Without our fear of death thought form we would be more aware of our past and probable lives (at least the feeling of them, if not the actual thought forms) as well as of the feelings of other people. We'd be able to feel them as our own feelings, as infants do. And thus we'd lose much of our sense of separatedness. That's how lunatics and magicians live: they still have individual lives, things happen to them, but there's less of a difference between something happening to them or to someone else. Something which happens to them is no more important than something which happens to someone else. Their feelings are no more important to them than someone else's feelings.

Death is the blank screen upon which all of our lifetimes are painted. Those lives don't exist; they're just momentary plays of light and shadow. However, to us they seem utterly fascinating and absorbing. To get to who we really are we would have to pull all of that obsession (energy pinned down by importance) out of all of those lives. As we do this, we find less and less of what we now consider to be "ourselves". We find the barriers which separate us from other people and the world around us becoming less and less distinct. It becomes harder for us to feel where we end and the next guy begins.

Death is just a way we keep score, keep count, keep track of things: it's how we separate this moment from that one, and this lifetime from that lifetime, and me from you. Without death the whole thing would just be one big stew. Death is what props "us" up – if it were not for death we would not have any sense of there being an "us" there at all. After all, what are "we" anyway? The sum total of all our experiences (memories) and expectations (desires). Right? What else is there? Nothing, right?

We, of ourselves, are absolutely nothing. Zero. All we are is something that is going to die. That's the only reason we have life at all, is to die. We are something that death conjured up, as an afterthought, to give itself a raison d'etre. And then, once it created us, we took off like a lumbering Frankenstein monster, and death tagged along to watch what we did.

All death is doing is watching us. It doesn't approve or disapprove of what it sees; it isn't conscience or shame; it just watches dispassionately. And what we are is death watching itself. It has nothing to do with us whatsoever. We are just a reflection in death's mirror – a symbol for death. We have no primary awareness: just as the moon only reflects light, we only reflect (are a symbol of) death's awareness of itself. We only exist as death is watching itself through the metaphor of our lives.

And that's why we say that death is mind: because that sense that we have that we are being watched is our death watching us. Without our death there watching us, we are nothing – nothing but a little point on a random walk through an infinite jungle in which nothing makes any sense whatsoever – there is no rhyme nor reason to anything (no mind). Mind (order) can only exist when there is something there watching the path that this random blip on the screen is taking. And that's what we call death.

BOOKS BY BOB MAKRANSKY:

*   *   *   *   *   *   *

Magical Almanac
http://groups.yahoo.com/group/MagicalAlmanac

is Bob Makransky's ezine of astrology and magic for thoughtful, intelligent people who are seeking something deeper than the usual New Age – astrological fare. To subscribe send an e-mail to:
MagicalAlmanac-subscribe@yahoogroups.com

*   *   *   *   *   *   *

http://www.DearBrutus.com – is Bob Makransky's personal website offering his books; astrology services; instructions on how to channel spirit guides and how to run past life regressions; free downloadable Mayan Horoscope software; information on the natural treatment of cancer and AIDS; articles on astrology, magic, Mayan folklore; humorous short stories, cartoons, and lots, lots more!

*   *   *   *   *   *   *

Bob Makransky's **Introduction to Magic** Series:

"In this series, not only do we get an author who knows his subject inside out, but also a directness of approach often not seen in works of this kind. Not for Makransky the wishy-washy approach that attempts to soothe and reassure the reader with false promises of magical success - something about which many customer complaints arise on the Amazon website - but, rather, an honest and uncompromising study of what Magic really entails. – James Lynn Page (author of *Celtic Magic*, *Everyday Tarot* and *The Christ Enigma*)

What is Magic?, the introductory book on witchcraft, can be sampled and purchased at:
Paperback $17.95: **http://www.createspace.com/4780367**
ebook $9.95: **www.smashwords.com/books/view/132491**
Kindle edition: **www.amzn.com/B0079K8X9O**

Magical Living, about paganism, can be sampled and purchased at:
Paperback $14.95: **http://www.createspace.com/4780358**
ebook $9.95: **www.smashwords.com/books/view/22860**
Kindle edition: **www.amzn.com/B0041843ZU**

Thought Forms, about cognitive psychology and the Mercury cycle, can be sampled and purchased at:
Paperback $19.95: **https://www.createspace.com/4770114**
ebook $9.95: **www.smashwords.com/books/view/22859**
Kindle edition: **www.amzn.com/B00439H1F6**

The Great Wheel, about reincarnation and the lunar cycle, can be sampled and purchased at:
ebook $9.95: **www.smashwords.com/books/view/306020**
Kindle edition: **www.amzn.com/B00CD958PS**

*   *   *   *   *   *   *

Volume I of Bob's Introduction to Magic series:

What is Magic?

Magic is a spiritual path which is not very well understood in our society. This is because the theory and practice of magic have never before been explained clearly and convincingly, in a way that makes sense to intelligent and thoughtful people. Written in a sassy, irreverent style, *What is Magic?* discusses how such otherworldly concepts as demons, casting spells, and bewitching are just the hidden underside of everyday society – the skeletons in everybody's closet. *What is Magic?* answers the questions which all serious spiritual seekers, no matter what their spiritual path, ask at one time or another, but can never find satisfactorily answered:

1) What is the difference between faith and fooling yourself?

2) What is the relationship between altered states and normal, everyday life?

3) If you lose your desires, as many spiritual paths advocate, what zest or spice does life have left?

4) If the world is an illusion or dream, as it's said to be, then why does it seem so real?

5) Where does the world of magic – the shaman's world – take off from the world of everyday life? What and where is the interface?

6) Why is it so difficult to achieve real, permanent spiritual growth?

"Bob is daring, willing to be offensive with his truths, and wise in the ways of words and magic. ... Bob Makransky, I feel, has written a great treatise on magic. I urge you to enjoy it as much as I have." from the foreword by Michael Peter Langevin, publisher of *Magical Blend* magazine.

Contents:

Spirits, Intent, The Nature of Reality, Spells, Charms & Rituals, Science Debunked, Demons, The Nature of the Self, Bewitching, Magic & Money, Death, Black Magicians & Vampires, Power Places, The Magician's God, Magical Time, Magic and Morality, Dreaming & Stalking, Magic and Sex.

"There is a certain no-nonsensical feel to his presentation that is both refreshing and a bit disconcerting. Makransky's writing style is very different from other New Age authors, and that alone should appeal to readers looking for a bit more substance in their study of magic" – J Byrne, *Psychic-Magic* magazine

What is Magic? 202 pages Paperback $17.95:
https://www.createspace.com/4780367
ebook $9.95 can be sampled and purchased at:
https://www.smashwords.com/books/view/132491
Kindle edition: **https://www.amzn.com/B0079K8X9O**

Volume III of Bob's Introduction to Magic series

Thought Forms

Astronomical and astrological explanations of Mercury's synodic cycle – its cycle of phases as it circles the sun, with tables 1900-2050.

Complete delineations for Superior and Inferior Conjunction, Greatest Eastern and Western Elongation, Stationary Retrograde and Direct, and their intervening phases in the natal, progressed, and transiting horoscopes.

Explanation of the astrological / magical view of mind (the theory of Thought Forms): what consciousness is, how it arose, and whither it is going.

Basic course in white magic with detailed instructions on: How to Channel and Banish Thought Forms; Creative Visualization; How to banish the Black Magicians in everyday life; How to Cast out Demons; How to use Tree Spirits.

"Bob Makransky is a knowledgeable, purposeful and entertaining writer." – Paul F. Newman, *The International Astrologer* magazine

"Steady Diamond Fire *readers are well acquainted with the genius of Bob Makransky. Highly recommendable."* – Joseph Polansky, *Diamond Fire* magazine

"Readers have become familiar with [Makransky's] fresh insights into different facets of astrology. In this book Thought Forms *he is especially provocative and I strongly recommend its purchase and study."* – Ken Gillman, *Considerations* magazine

"I will fully agree with the statement that 'You've never read a book like this before!' The material is fresh and woven very skillfully to conclusion. I look forward to his next installment of the trilogy." – Marion MacMillan, *SHAPE*

An indispensable reference you'll consult every time you read a chart!

Thought Forms Paperback $19.95 from:
https://www.createspace.com/4770114
Thought Forms ebook $9.95 can be sampled and
purchased at: **www.smashwords.com/books/view/22859**
Kindle edition: **https://www.amzn.com/B00439H1F6**

*   *   *   *   *   *   *

Volume IV of Bob's Introduction to Magic series:

The Great Wheel

*"On the afternoon of October 24ᵗʰ, 1917, four days
after my marriage, my wife surprised me by attempting
automatic writing. What came in disjointed sentences, in
almost illegible writing, was so exciting, sometimes so
profound, that I ... offered to spend what remained of life
explaining and piecing together those scattered sentences."*
– William Butler Yeats

It is often said in spiritual literature that time and space
are an illusion, *maya, samsara*. But what exactly does this
mean? And what implications does it have for how you
should live your everyday life? *The Great Wheel* is an
explanation of the System of birth, death, and rebirth which
Nobel laureate William Butler Yeats' described in his
masterpiece, *A Vision*.

Starting out with a discussion of how you can connect
with your true purpose in this life – the reason why you
incarnated on the earth at this time – *The Great Wheel*
describes simple techniques you can use (such as past life
regressions, probable reality progressions, and recapitulation
of present life memories) to glimpse different facets of your
Daimon (your oversoul; the totality of who you are), in order
to understand clearly how you got to where you are at right
now. To live your true life's purpose rather than drift along
helplessly, it is necessary to see how your present life situation
is the end result of decisions which you, yourself, made in
other lifetimes and realities.

An in-depth discussion of twenty-eight personality
types (depending upon where you were born in the moon's

monthly cycle of phases) illuminates your individual true purpose in incarnating in this life, and helps you to understand where you belong and where you are going.

The *Great Wheel* concludes with a fascinating explanation of what reality is all about: Mind and Memory, Waking and Dreaming, Change, Familiarity, and the Akashic Records.

"This new work in Bob Makransky's excellent and thought provoking 'Introduction to Magic' series ... is a fascinating and illuminating take on the meaning of the Moon. It's truly a Moon book unlike any other and is guaranteed to alter your perception of yourself and the world." – Paul F. Newman, author *LUNA: The Astrological Moon*

"Bob Makransky ... is directing the reader to access the higher consciousness. He gives many wonderful techniques for it . ... This is not the kind of book you just read and it's finished. It's really a work book. You have to practice the exercises he gives. You have to apply the lunar phases to your own chart and to others. Many statements require thought and reflection. Not beach reading material. Be prepared to be educated and also shocked!" - Joseph Polansky, *Diamond Fire* magazine

"It is difficult to change thought patterns to find a new path, and that is the primary reason I read The Great Wheel *and encourage others to read it. ... To use a 1960's term, this is a heavy book. It is very deep, thorough and forces one to step back and start looking at the big picture. What picture of your life is in need of help? What aspect of your personality could use some help? This book has the tools to help you".* - Peggy Mathias, *Psychic-Magic* magazine

The Great Wheel ebook $9.95 can be sampled and purchased at: **www.smashwords.com/books/view/306020**
Kindle edition: **http://www.amzn.com/B00CD958PS**

Topics in Astrology

A delightful cornucopia of over three dozen essays on a wide variety of astrological topics ranging from practical, hands-on advice to technical issues to humor and satire. *Topics in Astrology* is chock-full of original tips and guidelines for experienced practitioners (it may be a bit advanced for beginners, but even they will find parts of the book fascinating).

Partial Contents:

The natal horoscopes of Philadelphia hippie guru-cum-murderer Ira Einhorn and polygamist Mormon guru-cum-murderer Ervil LeBaron are thoroughly analyzed; as is the abortive romance between Nobel laureate William Butler Yeats and the unattainable beauty Maud Gonne. Exhaustive, in-depth discussions of how transits, primary directions, and secondary progressions work are illustrated with scores of examples taken from the horoscopes of notables. How to use astrolocality (employing astrology to find favorable and avoid unfavorable places to live or visit) is described in detail. The traditional rules of horary astrology are examined and evaluated in the cases of the *Titanic* disaster and the Nixon resignation. The rules of electional astrology are illustrated in a chapter on how to pick winning lottery tickets. The validity of eclipses and comets is examined; and technical issues such as how house systems are constructed are discussed in depth. Oh yes – Bob pokes fun at astrology too, with convincing analyses of the natal horoscopes (including predictions which came true!) for a couple of fictional characters.

Topics in Astrology 312 pages paperback $19.95
order from: **https://www.createspace.com/5712718**
Kindle edition $9.99 from:
http://www.amazon.com/dp/B019NSBP4Y

Intermediate Level Textbooks on Horoscope Interpretation

Planetary Strength – a commentary on Morinus

An essential contribution to natal horoscope interpretation. Taking as its point of departure *Astrologia Gallica* by Jean Baptiste Morin de Villefranche (1583 - 1656), *Planetary Strength* explains the differences between the strengths conferred upon planets by virtue of their sign placements (celestial state); house placements (terrestrial state); and aspects (aspectual state). A detailed system of keywords is augmented by insightful "cookbook" interpretations for each and every planetary combination. The depth and quality of the analysis – as well as the hundreds of practical examples and tips – make *Planetary Strength* an essential reference work which both neophyte and experienced practitioners will consult every time they read a horoscope.

"The book is beautifully written. With Makransky, whether you agree or disagree is not the issue - you will always get a good read. It is clear. He has done his homework. He makes the genius of Morinus accessable to English speakers. He shows us how to 'think astrologically'." – Joseph Polansky, *Diamond Fire* magazine

"What's fascinating about Planetary Strength *is that the author is using his own prose to describe the planets' conditions. In the introduction, he advises readers to study Morinus, but clearly Makransky's efforts are the better source. ... Try them in practice and compare these interpretations to what you might otherwise think about a planet. It may just sharpen your ability to make accurate statements about character, a person's history, and even to make predictions. And what more do you ask of astrology?"* – Chris Lorenz, *Dell Horoscope* magazine

"This is certainly an interesting addition to reading and interpreting the translations of Morinus' original work. It is detailed and considered, and the author's knowledge and experience are evident throughout." – Helen Stokes, *AA Journal*

"Presenting a mixture of discussion, detailed cookbook offerings and chart examples as well as keywords and tables, this fascinating book also addresses the fixed stars. ... This fascinating book assumes a fair knowledge of astrology as well as some experience in preparing charts." – Margaret Gray, *ISAR*

"This is a book that every beginner as well as advanced student of astrology would do well to possess. The author is extremely perceptive in his descriptions of the planets in their various strength and weaknesses ... this book would be a helpful aid to the researcher, as it would point him in the right direction." – Wanda Sellar, *Correlation*

Published by Wessex Astrologer - Bournemouth - UK
Planetary Strength 130 pages paperback £11.99
from: **https://www.amzn.com/1902405501**

Listen to Bob discuss *Planetary Strength* at:
http://www.myspiritradio.com/celebrity-profile?celeb_id=738

*   *   *   *   *   *   *

Planetary Hours

The Planetary Hours are an ancient astrological system for selecting favorable times to act (and avoiding unfavorable times), by assigning planetary rulers to the twenty-four hours of the day. This book has easy-to-follow instructions for finding your birthday and birth hour rulers, and clearly explains how these determine your personality and your luck. A chapter on electional astrology explains how to use the Planetary Hours to find lucky times to act (to ask for money; to ask someone on a date or to marry; to go on a journey; to begin a new business). The chapter on How to Cast Spells gives the low-down on how to make magical spells (and prayers) *really* work, using simple astrological techniques. The use of the Firdaria, an ancient astrological prediction system which indicates positive and negative periods during a lifetime, is illustrated with a detailed analysis of events in the life of Theodore Roosevelt. Complete Tables of Planetary Hours at the end of the book allow you to find favorable times to initiate activities for any day of the year, and for anywhere on earth from the Equator to 58° North and South latitudes.

"Bob Makransky ... describes Planetary Hours (PH) as the 'astrology of luck' and a method of finding empowering life moments for the proper exercise of freewill – to be yourself and not an enslaved cog of convention – Makransky explains in this admirably lucid guide book. As an introduction, this book is highly accessible." – AA Journal

"Bob Makransky has written the definitive book on Planetary Hours. It's the best book on the subject out there. It will be read and studied by future generations of astrologers. It's not just something that you read and discard. You want it in your bookshelf to refer to again and again." – Joseph Polansky, *Diamond Fire* magazine

Published by Wessex Astrologer - Bournemouth - UK
Planetary Hours 118 pages paperback £11.00
from: **https://www.amzn.com/1910531057**

*   *   *   *   *   *   *

Planetary Combination

Planetary Combination picks up where *Planetary Strength* left off, explaining how the planetary influences combine in aspects and configurations to paint a picture of a person and his or her life. Descriptions of planetary configurations such as Grand Trines, Grand Squares, T-Crosses, Wedges, Fans, Rectangles, Kites, and Trapezoids provide overall schematics of people's psychological dynamics. Then, detailed interpretations for the conjunctions, sextiles/trines, squares, oppositions, parallels/contraparallels, and Mutual

Receptions between the individual planets enable the practitioner to see clearly how these dynamics work out in a particular horoscope. An illuminating chapter on planetary conjunctions with the moon's nodes reveals the underlying karmic influences at work. An indispensable reference you'll consult every time you read a chart.

"Bob Makransky follows the dictum that "character is destiny" in Planetary Combination, *a detailed reference that allows the astrologer to make predictions based on what is revealed in the natal horoscope. While this book is nominally a series of explanations about aspects between the traditional planets, the degree of character description for each planetary pair is extraordinarily precise. An entire personality is captured within these aspects. In the same way that the author provides highly detailed character sketches for each planetary duo, he gives the same attention to configurations. In addition to the most common shapes, he also provides several pages on shapes that are not found in any other astrology text. An unusually terse and bold reference,* Planetary Combination *transcends psychological mumbo-jumbo to give you the bare-naked reality of the adult Western psyche."* - Chris Lorenz, *Dell Horoscope magazine*.

*"*Planetary Combination *is an excellent and comprehensive summary of all the relevant chart factors. ... One has to search hard to find such material! But this is all presented, as is all of Makransky's work, with vigour, wisdom and accessibility. ... Much of the book is taken up – as we might expect – with a very generous coverage of the astrological aspects. I looked up a few of my own and they were spot on. ...* Planetary Combination *fills a gap in the current state of astrological literature. It manages to retain both a sense of firm tradition whilst feeling utterly new and fresh."* – James Lynn Page, author of *Everyday Tarot, Celtic Magic, The Christ Enigma* and *The New Positive Thinking*.

"This is one of the best books on aspects out there. He not only deals with aspects themselves, but goes deep into chart morphology. It is one thing to analyze aspects and quite another to look at the "pictures" - the forms - that the aspects make. Most books on aspects deal with the aspects of longitude. But he also includes the parallels and contra-parallels. He has an interesting discussion of orbs, values (strengths of an aspect) and mutual receptions. A student would have to read many books from many authors to get the information that is given here. As always with Bob Makransky's work, the book is interesting and well written, not for a beginner or casual reader, but fascinating nevertheless - especially for a serious student." – Joseph Polansky, *Diamond Fire* magazine

Published by Wessex Astrologer - Bournemouth - UK
Planetary Combination 232 pages paperback £17.50
from: **https://www.amzn.com/1910531103**